Leadership Levers

Diana Jones has managed something few others can claim – merging rigorous research with highly pragmatic and specific advice for leaders. Leaders who dedicate themselves to learning what she has to teach will not only immediately improve the likelihood of success, but they will be more capable in virtually any future situation. Rarely does a book offer advice, the rationale for the advice, and tell the reader what to do when things go awry. This book should be on every leader's desk, read and re-read because the first reading will provoke change and second allow deep understanding.

– **Constance Dierickx**, *Ph.D., The Decision Doctor®*

Diana Jones helps us to see the invisible cords of leadership - it's not the job title or mastery of content that matters, but mastery of relationships. This book is full of insights into how we can better understand and dramatically influence the interpersonal dynamics of the leadership challenge.

– **Murray Sherwin**, *Former Chair of the New Zealand Productivity Commission*

Leadership Levers *is a landmark book. Diana Jones makes the invisible visible, slaughters the sacred cows of "engagement" and "consensus," and truly shows how to release untapped potential in organisations.*

– **Andrew Hollo**, Author of *From Impossible to Possible*

Diana compellingly articulates what we might intuitively know but struggle to describe. She makes the case for leadership of both the head and the heart, then methodically sets about explaining how to go about this - whether she is talking about navigating the complexity of multi-force stakeholder dynamics, the direct relationship between purpose and results, or shifting the way we should think about meetings. Insightful and pragmatic, Leadership Levers *stands out both new leaders and the experienced who are wondering why they are struggling to get results.*

– **Susan Freeman-Greene**, *CEO, Local Government New Zealand*

Leadership Levers

Releasing the Power of Relationships for Exceptional Participation, Alignment, and Team Results

Diana Jones

Routledge
Taylor & Francis Group

A PRODUCTIVITY PRESS BOOK

First published 2022
by Routledge
600 Broken Sound Parkway #300, Boca Raton FL, 33487

and by Routledge
2 Park Square, Milton Park, Abingdon, Oxon, OX14 4RN

Routledge is an imprint of the Taylor & Francis Group, an informa business

© 2022 Diana Jones

The right of Diana Jones to be identified as author of this work has been asserted by her in accordance with sections 77 and 78 of the Copyright, Designs and Patents Act 1988.

Library of Congress Cataloging in Publication Data

A catalog record has been requested for this book

ISBN: 9780367765194 (hbk)
ISBN: 9780367765187 (pbk)
ISBN: 9781003167334 (ebk)

DOI: 10.4324/9781003167334

Typeset in Minion
by Deanta Global Publishing Services, Chennai, India

Contents

Foreword

I've been to the remote beaches of Bora Bora and the crowded streets of Mexico City. My work has included governors, CEOs, business owners, athletes, educators, and the occasional college president. All of these diverse people in varied climes have a distinct commonality: They function for better or worse through relationships.

Every business is a relationship business today because John Naisbitt had it right four decades ago when he talked about "high tech/high touch" in his seminal book, *Megatrends* (1982). In this world of artificial intelligence, tele-health, robotics, and autonomous cars, you may think the high touch aspect has diminished.

Ironically, it is more needed than ever. That's why there are "live chats" on many company web sites, where you can talk in real time to someone who can solve your problems in a moment. The new sales reality is that evangelism—peer-level reference—is obsolescing the traditional sales forces. (If you think about it, St. Paul was probably the first viral marketer about two millennia ago.)

Diana Jones understands this and has written about the power of relationships in any business, under any circumstances. But it's not what you may think. Relationships are often ephemeral, a smile remaining where the Cheshire Cat used to be. They often rely on the unspoken and thrive on the unseen. This isn't magical, it is rather magnificent.

The sad part is that the leverage of relationships, internally with employees and externally with customers, isn't completely appreciated. If they were, they wouldn't go wrong so often. We search for blame instead of cause, look for excuses instead of accepting accountability.

Our insistence today on "identity" as some kind of marker or differentiator doesn't create common ground but rather common animosity. Our polarization is the result of trying to safeguard ourselves rather than foster relationships, to covet our group instead of welcoming others.

Think about it: Friendliness, generosity, encouragement, thoughtfulness, and similar qualities draw people and create trust, despite identity with gender, race, religion, or origin. And these sterling qualities aren't worn on the lapel like a merit badge or indicator or rank. Rather they are *felt* more than seen, *appreciated* rather than negotiated.

Diana allows the reader to understand the power of private experiences which can be shared, and shared experiences which can be personalized. That's quite an accomplishment, and that's why *Leadership Levers* should provide you with power and influence and, most importantly, the ability to help.

After all, it was Archimedes who said, "Give me a lever and I can move the world."

—Alan Weiss, Ph.D.
Author of Fearless Leadership, Million Dollar Consulting,
and over 60 other books in 15 languages

Acknowledgments

Just as it takes a village to raise a child, this book has resulted from encouragement and wisdom from my clients, peers, mentors, and friends. To my many clients who have trusted me to work with them and who then said yes when I asked if I might include elements of our work together in this book. Without their permission to share moments of triumph and challenges, their vulnerabilities, and daring, this book would not have come to life.

These people make up my village of trusted confidants and helpful wise guides.

A number of my long-time psychodrama mentors and colleagues discussed key areas or read the manuscript. Trainer, Educator and Practitioners, Dr. Charmaine McVea helped me express my ideas on intimacy and self-disclosure, Cher Williscroft offered the chance to talk through the intricacies of working with interpersonal conflicts, and Chris Hosking read the early chapters and invited me to expand my thinking on sociometric applications.

Financial advisor Chris Lee and I discussed essentials in the CEO and board governance relationships, and psychologist John Moffat and I discussed the dynamics of interpersonal understanding with human storytelling.

I would not have dared to become a writer if it were not for my long-time business mentor Alan Weiss who opened international doors for me and his community holds many of my long-time consultant and author peers. Alan introduced me to the practice of being a leadership advisor which freed me to offer my expertise to CEOs and senior leadership teams.

To my Pacific Rim Growth Group peers Andrew Hollo, Evan Bulmer, and Nicole Wilson from Australia, Steve Bleistein from Japan, Lisa Anderson and Jeff Gotro from the United States, and Jeff Skipper from Canada, many of whom I have yet to meet in person, but each has been inspired and determined to ensure we add greater value to our clients in our fortnightly zoom session with business coach Alan Weiss. Much of this development has been both personal and profound.

My wise friend and colleague Dr. Constance Dierickx from Atlanta who is miles away yet is available as if she is right next door. Linda Popky both colleague and editor who fine-tuned my manuscript with grammar and punctuation and made sure my ideas flowed. Consultant Simma Lieberman, the Inclusionist from San Francisco, and sociometrist Helen Phelan from Perth in Australia added to my knowledge of organization behaviors that exclude others.

Dr. Maris O'Rourke, writer, poet, and former Director of Education at the World Bank in Washington who sifted my near to final draft to final draft with her dedication to exquisite suggestions and clear expression.

My sincere thanks to Sharon Holmes who designed the diagrams in this book and tolerated the many refinements as my ideas took shape. Her artistry and precision executed with speed and grace.

About the Author

Diana Jones is a leadership advisor, executive coach, and author. She brings over 30 years of experience in leaders' behavioral change, working alongside public and private sector executives and professionals, as they reshape their relationships to achieve exceptional business results.

In 2020, she was the first New Zealander to be inducted into the Million Dollar Consulting Hall of Fame. She is a trainer, educator, and practitioner with the Australia Aotearoa New Zealand Psychodrama Association, and one of the few sociometrists in the world. She has strong international links with behavioral change consultants, trainers, coaches, and therapists.

Her work is described as *compelling, unique, inspiring, freeing, and impactful.*

CEOs and senior leaders call upon Diana for her insights and expertise when they want to reposition themselves, rapidly reconnect teams after restructures, transform organization cultures, and increase engagement with staff and stakeholders—all with a focus on delivering results.

Diana's first book *Leadership Material: How Personal Experience Shapes Leadership Presence* holds the keys to how leaders learn as they expand their influence and impact. Her work is quoted in *Forbes* and *CEO* magazines, and the *Huffington Post*.

Introduction

How many interactions and business meetings have you left feeling unsatisfied? You are not alone. We have people, a room to meet in, a start time, and an agenda. What could possibly go wrong? None of those things is wrong. They are all essential, but they are just not enough. These elements provide the infrastructure, but they don't take into account that people, their relationships, and interactions are central to productivity and success.

Early on in my professional life, I realized at conferences, training workshops, and meetings, it was the breaks and lunchtimes which were the richest source for getting to know people, learning, understanding how things work, and informing decision-making. This seemed back-to-front to me. I wanted to learn more of this phenomenon.

Understanding how groups work became a driving passion, as did making sense of the invisible dynamics governing why some people dominate, while others are content to be silent; why some people are listened to, and others were not. Why was it some groups have fun, others were competitive, or risk averse? I wanted to know how to create workable cultures in groups—cultures that reflect the organization's intention.

With my psychodrama trainers Dr. Max Clayton, Warren Parry, Lynette Clayton, Ann Hale, and Chris Hosking, I focused on sociometry, the art and science of relationships. I became fascinated with its language, concepts, and impact. What drew me in was that the content was peoples' lives and relationships, not facts and information. I saw the invisible become visible and made possible to interact with. What I saw and experienced was the movement of people drawing either toward or away from myself and one another. I saw how individuals' behavior created responses—connections, alliances, and schisms—which directly affected the group's success. I noticed that my personal development had immediate and profound impacts on my professional capacities.

I saw that being a companion on specific criteria was essential to belonging in any group, to being accepted, and to drawing in others. I wholeheartedly applied these methods and principles in my work in corporates and with leaders.

I discovered that social identity like leader, nurse, engineer, does not create common ground. In fact, it is more likely to create emotional distance, distaste, and rejection. Whether professional or sexual identity, race, religion, or country of birth, these shared social indicators often created unhelpful divisions of who was "in" and who is "out."

I discovered two more things:

- That it was the invisible personal qualities of being friendly, insightful, caring, and thoughtful expressed through behavior that drew people to one another, and
- That it was the invisible, deeply personal, and little-known private experiences which created emotional connections and increased vitality in groups.

What leaders seriously underestimate is that in every group, in every gathering, there are people with significant, private shared experiences. This is the true untapped source of brilliance, of exceptional contributions, of people's capacity to make a difference in the world.

From leading and being in groups for thousands of hours, I learned the principles and practices in relationship-building and producing helpful group dynamics that successful leaders can use. I saw the rapid and dramatic changes that executives and teams I worked with made in their businesses and in their careers.

I have written this book to enable leaders to mine the brilliance that often lies dormant and untapped within their organizations. Readers will have the principles and tools to go beyond the agenda, to truly engage with those around them, and release untapped capacities within their organizations. People will want to be led by them because of this.

Chapter 1 goes beyond job title and dives into the invisible yet personal behaviors that create leaders' abilities to draw people to them: self-disclosure, vulnerability, authenticity, and work relationship intimacy which provides meaning for others. Chapter 2 asserts the fad of engagement surveys measure the wrong things. Becoming familiar with the sociometric term "tele," the interpersonal flows of feeling that once mastered, helps shift organizations from individuals driving the business agenda in silos to groups working collaboratively. Clear descriptions of defensive behaviors and behaviors which draw people to contribute are given.

Chapter 3 champions distance and closeness as the real measure of health in relationships. Knowing where you stand in relation to key others is an invaluable perception measure for leaders with their relationship efficacy. Chapter 4 shifts attention to the art of reading people rather than content and the harsh consequences of failing to learn this aspect of organization life. Chapter 5 brings to our line of sight the previously invisible informal networks of relationships which describe how people work together. The formal organization chart indicates the power, authority, and decision structures, yet it is informal, personal, and usually private interactions based on specific criteria and choice, which both feed people's social and psychological needs and dictate what is done and how.

Chapter 6 propounds the power of purpose over habit for leaders' interactions, and Chapter 7 outlines principles and processes needed for leaders to produce meetings that participants both find deeply satisfying and that they give their best contributions. One of the big mistakes leaders and their teams make is assuming they have to give up their differences in order to gain alignment in direction. Chapter 8 documents tools of the trade for leaders which uncover new territory for discovering common ground, and how to let this become the source for alignment. We throw aiming for consensus out the window. We explore the tools to work well with the non-binary nuances inherent in a leader's everyday decision-making. Chapter 9 opens the door for leaders' own participation in groups and identifies the multiple avenues they have to influence. Chapter 10 champions personal development as the key to professional competence, and encourages readers to take immediate action.

1

Having the Top Job Doesn't Make You the Leader

Practically everyone agrees that leadership is an essential ingredient for business success. How to achieve great leadership is a matter of debate.

Millions of dollars are poured annually into leadership development programs, coaching, and training, yet there is a gap between where we'd like our leaders to be and where they actually are today.

That's because we've been looking in the wrong places and measuring the wrong metrics to assess leadership success. Two pivotal factors have been overlooked:

- The leader's capacity to engender purposeful staff participation
- Their ability to gain alignment for successful implementation of their vision and direction

These two factors require specific leadership processes and mindsets.

How do leaders shift from swimming with their heads full of good intentions to the place where they have the ability to release the full capacities of their group and deliver results? Let's start by identifying the main causes of disengagement and focus on what leaders can do to gain alignment.

Having the top job doesn't make you a leader. The social identity of a leader such as mechanic, doctor, nurse, teacher, marketer, African American, IT specialist, woman, banker, etc.—or any mix of these identities—gives no hint of the value and leadership capacities of that individual. Job titles may help people choose whom to consult for a specific matter and the types of decisions that person might make, but they don't convey leadership ability.

DOI: 10.4324/9781003167334-1

Many of us have naively expected that shared social identity would create unity. This helps to explain our penchant for conferences for the meeting of minds and sharing of experience. But, in fact, differentiating people by their social identity is one of society's most divisive tools. Continuing to differentiate by race, gender, ethnicity, or professional identity invariably leads to destructive behaviors, social and business exclusion, and restricted access to services rather than expansion.

That's because defining and separating groups by social identity attracts strong feelings from stereotyping and assumptions. Differentiating and creating hierarchies among groups by social identity underpins our social failures. As it turns out, academics, business schools, and leaders have been looking in the wrong place for unifying forces within society, organizations, and the groups we lead.

LOOKING FOR EGGS IN A SHOE SHOP

It's as if we've been looking for eggs in a shoe shop. No matter how carefully we look, it's unlikely we'll find them there between the sandals and the boots.

The real success of any leader lies in their identity—how they enact their role through their personal qualities. This deeply influences how people experience working with them, and impacts the results they achieve within their organization. The same is true for everyone else within the organization. Regardless of your appointed position, you can lead and be dramatically effective.

Organizations invest millions of dollars in training and development each year to provide leaders with skills and expertise in strategic and business planning, business analysis, performance management, and negotiation. Yet it's the leader's capacity to produce progressive interaction among people and release both the known and hidden talents of others that is key to that leader's success.

Our commitment to linear solutions to leadership development has not produced the results envisioned, yet we have persisted down that path as if we are still looking for those eggs in that shoe shop. Business schools, academia, and leadership advisors still hold onto the belief that a focus on developing specialist content, logic, and information will help leaders align people. It doesn't. These activities may fill leaders' minds, but they do little to help them develop inspiring relationships that bring the best out of people.

Early in my career, I was program manager, then course director, for the New Zealand College of Management. My function was to design (and at times lead) month-long leadership development programs.

The Advanced Leadership Program emerged from war times at an administrative staff college in the 1950s. By the mid-1980s, the program was tired—so much so that the retired CEOs who were the course directors were known to fall asleep during working sessions. Forty middle and senior executives would attend the month-long program and endure a series of presentations. Working groups met in the evenings and proceeded to run up horrendous bar bills.

After enduring one of these programs, I implemented changes. First, I modified the welcome meeting to focus on building connections among participants. Each executive set personal learning goals. We formed and embedded peer groups of six to seven participants based on the criteria, *With whom here would you choose to solve complex problems?* The self-selection of peer group members was a critical success factor.

Each session leader was invited to implement an interactive two- to three-day session using a variety of learning methods. During the final three days, I embedded a current case study with a nationwide organization, which concluded with a live report back to the CEO.

Remarkably (but not unexpectedly), alcohol consumption dropped below 50% of previous programs. Evenings were largely working sessions and peer-group interactions. Life-long collegial friendships were formed.

Over successive months, I introduced 360-degree feedback, two-day looking glass business simulation from the Center for Creative Leadership in North Carolina, and personalized coaching.

These innovations in the 1980s dramatically expanded the College's reputation. I saw firsthand how the power of relationships among participants contributed directly to the development of these senior leaders, their participation in the program, and their subsequent professional contributions. Month-long intensive leadership development programs have long since disappeared but the lifelong collegial relationships made in those times did not.

How often have you gone to conferences only to find the real source of learning, insight, and vitality was found during breaks and mealtimes?

Interpersonal connections, happenstance meetings, and complementary experiences are discovered within personal interactions, rather than during the sessions that impart content and knowledge. A simple question like, *What brought you here?* might well begin a lifelong collegial friendship. *I nearly didn't come, my Dad is very ill* might create an empathetic response and simple human connection. I wanted to discover how to bring relevant human connections into working sessions, where participants got to know one another rapidly and relevantly, and could bring their authentic selves to the work of the group.

I was determined to make this the emphasis of my work with clients. I wanted to help leaders get the best from those with whom they were working. I wanted leaders and presenters to give up the relentless one-way delivery of information—either verbally or by endless PowerPoint slides—with participants having no way to integrate or apply that information. From international regulatory standards agencies to community medical centers, leaders madly hoped that giving information and ideas was the best way to generate participation and alignment among participants. They thought this would ensure changes are implemented and innovative developments flourish. But there was a problem: one-way communication just doesn't work.

Gillian Mylrea, veterinarian, Head of Standards Department at the World Organisation for Animal Health (OIE), grappled with this. She was facilitating a three-day seminar with participants from 24 countries to ensure they took on:

- Understanding their responsibilities as a Member of the OIE
- Improved animal health and welfare worldwide
- Prevented the spread of pathogenic agents via international trade
- Enhanced access to global markets for animals and animal products
- Avoided unjustified sanitary barriers to trade
- Participated in the OIE's standard-setting process

This was no mean feat. This particular session was held in Nairobi, Kenya. Gillian and I discussed her strategy. Having worked previously with me in New Zealand, she wanted participants to truly engage with one another as they grappled with their broad agenda. She had researched how adults learn and was convinced that her organization would have a stronger and more consistent uptake of new policies if delegates engaged with one another rather than merely absorbed information.

Historically, the seminar format included many presentations and little time for interpersonal interactions. Gillian had noticed few people interacted in the breaks. We settled on a different approach.

To begin the seminar, Gillian's invitation was for participants to meet one another. They were invited to stand in a large circle and introduce themselves with their name, role, and country. Gillian then asked, *Who has been to five or more of these events? Please step forward ...,* then step back again. Then, *Who has been to between two and four of these events? Please step forward ...,* then back again. Finally, *Who is here at their first OIE event?* Immediately, everyone had a picture of the group's depth of experience with OIE events, and also who the newcomers were.

Delegates were then invited to choose three other people they had yet to meet to make a group of four and to let one another know one thing they were looking forward to in the next three days. She suggested they take 15 minutes to do this.

The noise level went through the roof. As Gillian looked around, she saw the delegate's animation and vitality. She saw these professionals and specialists deeply engaged with one another. She invited participants to continue interacting during the coffee break and 30 minutes later, most of the group were still talking animatedly in small groups. This was Gillian's vision: a seminar with participants deeply engaged with one another on what was important to them.

This shift from using the formal social identity of name, role, and country led to participants discovering shared interests, common ground, and different perspectives on similar challenges. The real work of this OIE seminar was underway.

The real source of leaders' success resides in their capacities and not in their skills, abilities, and expertise. It is their ability to:

- Be succinct and have clear expectations
- Produce relevant interactions among people
- Draw out stories and experiences that create interpersonal connections
- Stimulate networks of relationships that facilitate exceptional work being done

I want leaders everywhere to be able to access the capacity to tap into the interests and concerns of their groups as a lever to enable their people to connect rapidly and relevantly.

I've discovered working with leaders and their relationships dramatically impacts business performance, creates a sense of belonging, and enhances professional identity. Failure to adequately do this ensures that many meetings and day-to-day interactions with leaders are boring, and barely fit for purpose.

WHEN THE EGGS HAVE PASSED THEIR USE-BY DATE

We have accepted that such mechanical functions as introducing one's self to new groups with your name and role are helpful—but they rarely are. What *is* helpful is to include personal information in your introduction. Three options are:

- The qualities you bring to achieving the meeting's outcome
- The experience you bring that does the same
- Why this meeting is important to you or your organization

Leaders who invest in discovering exactly who is at the table know the specific individuals present are more important than any role.

For years, leadership experts have extolled leaders to invest in their people, but this investment has usually been focused on skill-building and introducing new tools and techniques. This rarely helps.

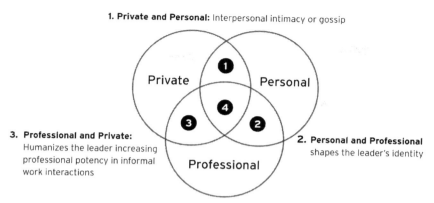

1. Private and Personal: Interpersonal intimacy or gossip

Private

Personal

3. Professional and Private: Humanizes the leader increasing professional potency in informal work interactions

2. Personal and Professional shapes the leader's identity

Professional

4. Private, Personal and Professional is the source of authenticity, trust, intimacy and vulnerability

FIGURE 1.1
The three elements of intimacy

The right place for relationship investment is in quite a different territory. The focus should be on the personal aspect of professional development—building leaders' capacities for relationships, how to lead groups, and how to create a culture of purposeful participation.

Most organizations and leaders make the mistake of separating personal and professional development. Leaders who encourage professionals to keep their personal lives separate and private from their professional lives are making a fundamental mistake. First, leaders (or anyone else) cannot successfully compartmentalize their personal life. They may try to place it in the background of their identity as leader, but personal lives have a way of influencing our professional identity (Figure 1.1).

Harry was a high flying bank executive and caring father of three small children. The day before he was to present to a board meeting, he came to work with a black eye. It turns out he had begun a romantic relationship with one of his direct reports. Both had decided to leave their respective partners and live together. That weekend, her aggrieved partner had come to the local café Harry favored, and hit him. Unwilling to fudge the situation, Harry let the CEO and board chair know exactly what had happened. His disclosure was private and personal. His vulnerability was refreshing and pragmatic.

Experiences in one's personal life at times reduce the capacity to respond to organizational change—underpinning interpersonal conflicts, and possibly leading to job loss. The professional and emotional stress is too frequently siphoned off privately to an Employee Assistance Program or corporate counseling. Often this service is limited to just a few sessions, which is rarely enough to address significant personal trauma and loss. How we respond to loss and trauma is precisely what makes us human.

Most leaders fear the emotional aspect of personal traumas being excessively expressed—tears, frustrations, anger—and rightly so. Relentless emotional expression devoid of thinking and action doesn't fit with work cultures. This belongs instead to personal friendships, family intimacy, trusted collegiality, and therapy.

When one of these factors excessively dominates, that leader will be out of kilter with the work culture.

Leaders fear that delving into personal emotional outbursts will release the proverbial can of worms. They fear people's emotions will interfere with work getting done. Rightly so, this is accurate. When emotions dominate, thinking and action fall into the background. In Figure 1.1, gossip is the downside of leaders sharing other's private and personal information.

When leaders know the cause of unhelpful behaviors or emotional responses (both their own and others), thus meeting point 4 from Figure 1.1, they can draw on empathy and human kindness. The result is that the employee feels valued and work is done.

Ray, the general manager in a small medical manufacturing company, overheard one of his operations manager, Rob, shout at one of his peers. Rob had become deeply distressed, saying he was overwhelmed and couldn't cope. Ray knew Rob had taken on the care of his frequently ill and distressed mother. He guessed that might be the reason this was happening. By asking about this, he learned that Rob's early morning routine upset him deeply. He hated seeing his mother so helpless and his distress was carried over to his time on the job.

Ray proposed he and Rob discuss the priorities for the day. They agreed to a check-in each morning focusing on the same two areas each day: what was important for the day, and how Rob was to achieve that. Over the next few weeks, Rob's sense of achievement was refreshed, although he still had to manage his mother's illness. Ray's empathy and understanding of Rob's situation helped create a simple system to ensure the emotional stability of his staff while under intense pressure—without compromising the business focus.

The relevant sharing of personal and private experience is crucial to the development of human bonds, which in turn facilitate organizational work. Chapter 4 explores this phenomenon in greater depth.

Intimacy, vulnerability, and authenticity are close allies. All three include the capacity to let others know how you think and feel on important matters. All three relate to the relevant degree of personal self-disclosure. Self-disclosure is the information we give about ourselves, and can include both content and feeling. Vulnerable and authentic leaders dramatically increase their visibility through their capacity to create relevant intimacy in their relationships (Table 1.1).

Intimacy in work relationships is a process where recipients experience the leader's authenticity. The leader lets themselves be more known through simple self-disclosure, which in turn evokes thoughtful emotional responses. This draws people closer together aligned with their work purpose.

Let me be clear. Both *what* is shared and *how* it is shared are crucial to the success of leaders and organizations. Self-disclosure relates to the individual, and describes how this person is in relationship with others.

Intimacy, on the other hand, is two-way. Intimacy is developed within a relationship. The leader might act in a way that creates intimacy, but it is only created when the other responds in a way that develops a capacity between the two, or the group. If the other isn't receptive, or rejects the self-disclosure, discomfort results or the self-disclosure is experienced as inappropriate. Micro-managing and harassment are examples. Yet self-disclosure is where the gems lie. Successful leaders know how to create a relationship environment for employees to warm up to the relevant level of self-disclosure and maintain their working relationships.

In many of the groups I lead, initial interactions are based on getting to know one through simple storytelling. Leaders' stories are in response to bespoke criteria relevant to the group's purpose such as:

TABLE 1.1

Levels of Self-Disclosure

Level	Example	Leader's Purpose with Group
Simple	Personal Information, response Insight and/or reflection *Example l: I'm pleased to see you* *Example 2: I'm concerned this conversation is going around in circles. We have been here many times before*	Establish or reaffirm your relationship with the team
Deeper	Deeper disclosure in taking accountability of one's own actions—including the professional impact on themselves and/or the business *Example: I'm pulling my hair out with my executive team. They don't listen to one another and they refuse to collaborate. My staff sees the left hand doesn't know what the right hand is doing. We are on the edge of implementing our new strategy and I have lost confidence that we will be successful. Nothing I have tried has worked. What would you advise?*	Personal insights with intervention to redirect team efforts to align to vision/direction
Unguarded	Unguarded disclosure of one's imperfections with deep trust, risking rejection to reveal the personal heart of the matter, so people can see things from your perspective *Example: You won't hear me talking badly about any of you behind your backs. I'll stop that. I will be asking you. "How are you going and how can I help?" when I see you under pressure*	Reveal personal imperfections risking rejection, to create human connections aligned with business direction

- One of the most difficult situations you have led through and what you learned from that
- A turning point in your career and how that influences your leadership approach now
- What, or who is one of the most important influences in your life right now?

Our work is then underway. Executives share deeply from their life experience and the influence this has on them. Many of the stories are simple life events yet powerful in their telling. Typical examples are the death of a loved parent or staff member or exhaustion from an ongoing significant work challenge.

These are moments when the level of intimacy in a group deepens. To hold this level of intimacy within the group and to ensure the speaker is not isolated, I tend to expand the attention from the speaker to the responses of their peers. I base my approach on the premise the group is a system of relationships.

I invite group members to show their response in the moment. I do this by inviting peers to use distance as a measure of closeness. They will draw their chairs closer. At other times, I would invite people to stand closer in response, and then put words to what has drawn them closer. Online, I invite people to use an icon or the distance between their hands to reflect their movement toward the speaker.

As each leader responds, they use their own life experiences to relate to the speaker. They indicate their care for what is happening. With their relationships tacit, work conversations can then be at the heart of the matter with the usually complex work ahead of the group.

Without this consideration of interpersonal connections, work groups can fragment when the level of intimacy deepens, and the speaker is left isolated. The level of group anxiety rises and concentration on work matters falters.

Insight: Three simple principles for leaders are paramount in sharing formerly personal and private information with any work group:

1. **Be authentic**. This is the personal quality of being honest when you are with others. You are congruent in what you say and mean. Others might see you are shy, thoughtful, or that you are candid and speak your mind. The distinction here is you do not need to honestly say everything. Discerning what is important and what is not is crucial.
2. **Create connections within the group**. Self-disclosure creates openness or friendliness in collegial relationships enabling people to respond to one another more easily.
3. **Don't expect the group or anyone in the group to look after you**. Use your own support network of peers, friends, and family for this. The distinction here relates to building strong work groups. "Rescuing" undermines the effectiveness among leaders and their groups.

Four factors influence a leader's capacity for intimacy:

- How much they trust recipients to be respectful of what is shared
- Their courage to create new norms of interaction relevant to the current situation
- Having slightly less fear of rejection than desire and daring to get to the heart of the matter
- The ability to keep functional relationships around them

The main fear holding leaders back from being authentic is their fear of being rejected. The downside of leaders who consistently avoid intimacy is that they are perceived as either logical, guarded, inhumane, or defensive. The leaders' discomfort in revealing their thoughts and feelings is offset by the value of creating a group culture where both they and the participants are confident they are working at the heart of the matter.

The leaders' real agenda is established at the moment when they share a personal and private insight into their work with the team or individual. That's the moment when team members know they are trusted.

> A group of 30 senior executives from a range of organizations was exploring storytelling. We identified organization restructuring as a fraught area.
>
> I asked the group, *"How many of you here grew up with one parent?"* Half the group formed a subgroup. *"How many grew up with someone other than your parents?"* A smaller group formed. *"How many of you grew up with two parents?"* About a third of participants formed a subgroup. Several people were taken aback at the unexpectedly large group who had grown up with two parents.
>
> The ensuing conversation among a mix from each subgroup related links between their experiences growing up and their approaches to implementing organizational change. The simple level of self-disclosure enabled sharing of experiences, success stories, and lessons learned. Participants got to know one another at greater depth, while opening doors for future consultations.

I don't include the prior example as a method, but to show how appreciating others' experience contributes to a shared understanding of the likely source of different perspectives.

Tapping into intimacy in a relevant way, through the realm of personal and private experience, holds a rich source for leaders to build strong, unifying relationships among those that work for them. This requires accepting that our personal and professional lives are interwoven and affect each other. Successful leaders consciously choose to emphasize one or the other. The interactions leaders have with team members and staff dramatically improve when their mindsets include personal interactions. Leaders learn they really *can* be in at least two places at once. Chapter 9 expands on how to do this under Personal insights.

EMPATHY IS ONLY HALF THE STORY

The territory we are entering is empathy, but interpersonal empathy between two people is only part of the story. Empathy is the ability to understand and share the feelings of others and it's central to a leader's emotional intelligence.

The three interrelated areas of empathy are:

- **Cognitive empathy,** where leaders understand and can imagine how a person feels and what they might be thinking. In response to a colleague who missed a sought-after promotion: "How disappointed you must be. You gave this your all." Or "That's good. That wasn't the right role for you. This is a real turning point for you to find the right thing."
- **Emotional empathy,** where leaders share the feelings of another person. I vividly recall being in Rotorua, New Zealand, on the morning of September 11, 2001. I was about to lead a group retreat for 15 IT leaders. I watched the morning news in horror as two planes crashed into the World Trade Center in New York City. As I began to realize the extent of the devastation, I heard the then New York Mayor Rudy Giuliani say, "The numbers of casualties will be more than any of us can bear." His ability to accurately read and reflect on the situation in that moment helped everyone accept the shocking reality and take rapid action.
- **Compassionate empathy,** where leaders go beyond understanding to taking action to help where they can. CEO Evelyn decided to go with the Marines slogan "leave no one behind" plus "everyone needs mana

(respect) and money" as she and her leadership team implemented a dramatic downsize in response to changes in government priorities. They interviewed every person to help them out of the organization by finding out and funding what they really wanted to do. They created "care packages" which were as diverse as job training, mature apprenticeships, university, money, finding them a job elsewhere within the sector, small business loans, etc.—you name it they did it. Her VP operations totally got it and was brilliant. Evelyn went on to report a couple of years later that one of the most bitter managers ran toward her in the street—she recoiled—he threw his arms around her and said, "the best thing that ever happened to me was being kicked out by you."

What is too frequently overlooked is that empathy is one-way, from the leader to the others.

GROUP EMPATHY

A much overlooked yet core capacity for leaders is group empathy—the leader's capacity to read people and groups. The capacity to read the mood of a team or organization, and to know the unexpected things people hold close to their hearts at work, is a core competency for anyone working with groups. Learn to read the flow of feeling from groups with whom you work and you will have methods and processes to gain alignment and engagement as you produce exceptional results.

Within hours of the Christchurch mosque massacres in March 2019, New Zealand Prime Minister Jacinda Ardern was in Christchurch, wearing a hijab, and putting her arms around victims and their families. This simple act of human compassion—her inner value of "You are us" enacted through her role of leader—was powerful, heartfelt, and resonated both locally and internationally.

Ardern immediately read the silent anguished pleas of *Did you see what happen? Help us—we're hurt.* She rapidly vowed never to say the killer's name, and within days had banned military-style semiautomatics and assault rifles throughout New Zealand.

Ardern's ability to read and compassionately respond to the emotional experience of the massacre victims and their families stimulated an outpouring of national social compassion and pragmatic action on the vexing problem of easy access to automatic weapons.

Predicting stuff is hard. Polls are not able to read mood with any degree of accuracy. Trends are a source of possible futures. But what is crucial in reading any situation is a leader's capacity to read the mood—the emotional tone of their people. Thoughtful anticipation is crucial to leaders leading, creating engagement and alignment, and releasing the talents of those around them.

THE LEADER'S POWER TOOLS

Leaders often forget they are leaders of people, not subject matter experts or leaders of content. Leaders need to shift gears—from preparing content and using logic to preparing to tap into the experience and expertise of the people around them to get things done.

How often have you encountered silence and blank stares in response to your vision, when in fact people are reflecting, thinking of implications, and making sense of what is being asked of them? Consider that the audience likely doesn't know the rules of engagement. Just as leaders can learn how to work with groups, many people need to learn how to *participate* in groups. They just don't know.

Rather than being annoyed by the lack of response and the blank looks, strong leaders look into the gap, and see what they want to be there. Do you want to see people interacting, contributing, doing their best to solve problems, innovating, and making decisions which progress the business and enhance the experience of customers and stakeholders?

If yes, then this is the area in which to focus your learning. Just as leaders need to learn how to help their people participate, many people also need to learn how to participate in work groups. Too often the experiences people bring to groups derive from their family dining table, their culture, or educational experiences, none of which are a good fit for purpose in contemporary business settings.

Mena Antonino, a long-time colleague of mine, diversity coach, and facilitator to boards and leadership teams, eloquently describes this from her work.

As a board member you are expected to contribute, and to be heard. People are depending on your participation to make a contribution. This creates stress and barriers, as these expectations are so different from our cultural settings. Under stress, the tendency is to default back to what we know from our fono (any type of meeting between people including national assemblies and legislatures, as well as local village councils) cultural setting where as women our role is to receive instruction, and support the chief and matai: being quiet, being deferential, being respectful and humble, which mostly means "Say nothing. Know your place."

Antonio continues, "Pacific women's roles have changed in the world."[1] She adds,

three things build confidence;

- Prepare the one or two things you'll contribute that will move the *waka* (boat) forward
- Don't get caught in the "changing the world debate"
- Before the meeting, initiate and greet others to bring your voice into the room and yourself into the present moment

CONCLUSION

I have seen too many leaders think their role enables them to be great people leaders. They give presentations and lead meetings as though the people aren't important. They emphasize meeting administration rather than thoughtfully implementing tried and true behavioral processes to gain alignment. What leaders do and how they lead are as important as who they are. Any leader who separates their personal experience from positively impacting their professional life overlooks a major source of learning. Self-disclosure is a leader's wellspring of their personal authenticity and vulnerability. Chapter 2 identifies two sociometric terms *tele* and *criterion* among levers that leaders have to create for unity in their organizations. Leaders, you have a choice: you unite people or alienate them? The behaviors of both options are laid bare.

NOTE

1. Antonio, Mena. Interview.

2

Unity in the War Room

A leader's mandate is to unite a group of people who may have disparate agendas and to align them with the leader's vision, direction, and expectations, in order to achieve the desired results.

This sounds simple, yet two mistakes are often made. The powerful levers for purposeful communication are frequently forgotten, and too many leaders forget the critical next step—ensuring their decisions are properly implemented.

The recent fad of engagement surveys is not helpful. These surveys measure the wrong things. Leaders whose teams return low scores are shocked and downhearted, and they often don't know what to do with the results. They just know they want to connect better with those on their team. Effective leaders want to be closer to their teams, and their teams want to be closer to one another.

For years, Gallup surveys persisted in asking the question, *Do you have a friend at work?* The problem is friendship is nebulous and the answers to this question don't provide actionable information. Gallup would have hit pay dirt had they instead asked, *Do you have one or more confidants at work?* According to Carl Hollander, Sharon Hollander, and Ann Hale [1], confiding in a colleague and being chosen as a confidant are two of the nine criteria for choosing companions ensuring psychological safety.

Gallup's 2018 report notes that

> Over nearly two decades, the annual percentage of engaged U.S. workers has ranged from a low of 26% in 2000 and 2005 to the recent six-month high of 34% in 2018. On average, 30% of employees have been engaged at work during the past 18 years

[2].

DOI: 10.4324/9781003167334-2

The persistent glaring gap between leaders and their people is stark and laid bare.

What are leaders doing that ensures this gap continues to exist? It's a fantasy to think that people follow leaders only because of their rational, logical, or visionary approaches. People follow leaders because of their:

- Vision, direction, and results being sought
- Personal qualities
- The way these leaders make their staff feel about their work, themselves, and the organization

The experience people have working with a leader is the "glue"—the main attraction. Leaders create an emotional connection with those around them. The emotional experience is paramount, since emotional connections are the key to successful work relationships. The specific emotional experience we're referring to here is one of *companionship*.

The key to anyone's professional success lies in finding and choosing companions at work based on a range of critical criteria. These include choosing the right people to:

- Help solve problems
- Understand what's going on in the organization
- Allow them to say what they think
- Motivate and inspire them
- Share confidences
- Be on the lookout for when help is needed

Knowing who would drop everything for you when the chips are down gives people confidence. It's precisely this criterion that gives considerable grief when those you thought would back you don't actually do that. Misjudging how close someone is to you is the source of painful and insightful learning for many leaders.

LETTING GO OF OLD PARADIGMS

Imagine a war room filled with heads of government agencies, entrepreneurs, the heads of police, defense forces, and secret services, plus the chief of the President's or Prime Minister's staff. This immediately raises a problem. Who actually leads? There is the appointed meeting leader and agenda, yet more importantly, what identities do people take on in the meeting when they are all CEO equivalents? Who holds the key pieces of the puzzle the group wants to resolve? Who emerges as the key influencers?

Emphasizing names and roles in introductions belongs to the Dark Ages. These two facts are barely relevant in crises. What is relevant is that those gathered work well together. The lever to rapid progress is knowing the qualities and experience each player brings to the setting, and their trust in one another.

In Aotearoa, New Zealand, during the 2020 COVID-19 pandemic, Dr. Ashley Bloomfield, the CEO of the Ministry of Health, brought experience and expertise as a medical practitioner, seasoned public sector leader, public health specialist, former hospital CEO, and non-communicable disease prevention and control specialist with the World Health Organization (WHO).

Bloomfield's mutually trusted relationship with the Prime Minister of New Zealand, Jacinda Ardern, quickly became evident. For the first 48 days of the pandemic, both he and Prime Minister Ardern jointly led the daily 1 pm briefing.

Their continual fronting of daily media briefings reflected a two-fold unity of purpose:

- To detect and prevent virus spread in the community
- To maintain public trust and confidence

Both Ardern's and Bloomfield's relentless reliability, their ease with information, and their calm, respectful, and personable demeanors with journalists' questions immediately engendered trust and cooperation among the public.

Over the ensuing months, ample mistakes were made. The glaring gap between policy decision and pragmatic implementation in hospitals, general practices, and the health sector were laid bare on numerous occasions. From deficits in the personal protective equipment (PPE) supply chain to testing accessibility to managed isolation deficits, Bloomfield fronted every obstacle and saw that they were corrected.

Here are two leaders, one political and the other a senior official. They worked well together in their respective and distinctive roles under intense scrutiny.

In crises—whether fighting for freedom from invasion, the threat of extinction, or freedoms being threatened, diminished, or taken away—threats create unity of direction among those affected. Rooms full of leaders and experts draw together rapidly to strategize and take action to take care of those who are hurting. Communities draw together to protest, or push back. Individuals speak truth to power. They declare their resistance, stand against the common enemy, and come together to fight for their collective rights.

What happens in non-crisis times? What happens in times of development, innovation, and business as usual?

It's here that the gap between leaders and their staff are frequently revealed where managers:

- Operate in silos
- Attend to their business group over the interests of the wider business
- Fight over budgets, staffing, or recognition
- Are critical of or fail to help colleagues
- Duplicate efforts
- Create in-crowds and out-crowds
- Fail to develop their people
- Tolerate a dominant or absent leader

It's as if the team is stuck at storming within Bruce Tuckman's 1965 four stages of group development (forming, storming, norming, and performing) [3]. Business units flourish at the expense of groupwide success. Problems within the business unit are solved within—often at the expense of a colleague's business—and managers are frequently isolated from one another (Figure 2.1). The pressure for the leader to be expert, conflict arbiter, and decision-maker all at once is intense. Strategy development and implementation is challenging, as the group members don't know or don't care about the overall business success.

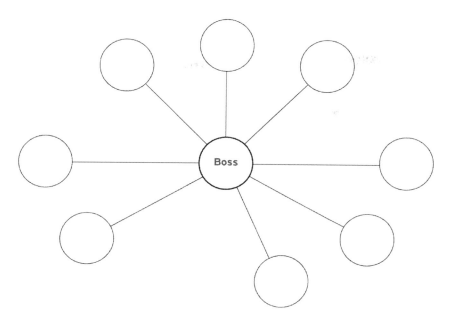

FIGURE 2.1
Leader-dependent siloes group

Tuckman's model is just that, a model albeit helpful. Most groups continually cycle through these four stages. They revert back with shifts in context, the addition of new members or leaders, or existing members or leaders leaving. The model is helpful in providing a shared framework for making an assessment for interventions.

It is in these gaps between leaders and their staff or among staff that the secret to leadership success lies.

WHAT IS IN THE GAP?

Interstitial space is the space between two entities. Think of a creature residing between two grains of sand. In tissue cells, the interstitial fluid provides the microenvironment that allows for the movement of ions, proteins, and nutrients across the cell barrier. Similarly, with interpersonal or intragroup relationships what is in the gap is invisible, yet can still be felt. This gap is where leaders should focus their attention. This is the territory leaders can master and mine for brilliance, and it's the central focus of this book.

Thoughtfully tuning into and reading their people allows leaders to craft a question that taps into four factors:

- A current central concern of the group
- The individuals' experience and expertise
- The capacity for differences to emerge
- An environment where group members learn more information about themselves as a group

The responses will release the sparks of interpersonal intimacy. Human connections are created and strengthened; stereotypes fall away. The alchemy of interpersonal connections is activated—releasing attributes, capacities, and capabilities which have previously laid dormant.

The leader and those they lead belong to a system of relationships. Yet the space between leaders and their people is where the action needs to be in ensuring the "right" relationships for work to be done.

The interstices between two people, among people, or between leaders and their team hold mutual positive flows of feeling. Mistakenly labeled "energy," a mutual flow of feeling among people creates the vibrancy felt by others. This flow of feeling is created by purposeful connections creating relationships among people. When relationships are underdeveloped, or absent, there is a cool or tense dynamic in the atmosphere. At times of unresolved interpersonal conflict, "you could cut the atmosphere with a knife."

The magnetic and perceptive CEO of a federal services organization noticed his leaders were not implementing the decisions made by his leadership team. The CEO knew his direct reports had strong relationships with one another and with their managers. If anything, they were overly protective of their staff. He decided to speak to this operational management team to discover what caused the lack of action. He was astonished there was little or no response to the vision he had outlined. Then it dawned on him. He'd been in his role for about a year. These people, many of whom had worked in the organization for ten years or more, didn't really know one another. The very thing that created a distance between the CEO and these managers was the distance between one another.

In this case, the interstitial space was like the Dead Sea.

Successful leaders look into the gap and have a vision of their staff interacting as they identify problems, collaborate and are cohesive, share different perspectives, and find innovative solutions.

Where goodwill flows among the players, warmth and vibrancy are apparent. The task of the players is to agree on the purpose of their interactions and produce interactions that generate mutuality. In short, leaders are responsible for ensuring interstices are ripe for productivity, and everyone can learn this.

But what is it that creates cohesion among people in organizations *and* has them productively focus on work?

What tools do leaders have to build cohesion?

DISCOVERING THE STRANGE ATTRACTORS IN GROUPS

Thinking systemically is a powerful tool for leaders. Using systems thinking, leaders can rapidly make assessments by trusting that:

- Unworkable behaviors will be repeated. There isn't a need to fret you won't act resourcefully. You can trust that the individual or group will repeat the behavior and you can respond at any moment should you want to do so.
- When you change one part of the system, your intervention affects the whole system. An overloaded IT help desk halved the time of their fixits when they undertook to speak calmly to agitated customers using their first names.
- Whatever you want to turn around or improve in your organization, systems thinking indicates that the behavior is most likely evident within your leadership team. With the example above, the IT leadership team didn't know the names of everyone in their group or

where they were located geographically. They simply hadn't bothered to learn who their staff were. This leadership team shifted from impersonal staff interactions to being personable.

These three principles are invaluable for leaders. They give leaders choices for intervening with individuals, their team, the company, or the timing of an intervention.

In my work with senior leadership teams over many years, they comprise subject matter experts and their leader, a Vice President or CEO. The team members are invariably sought after as a subject matter specialist and high-level government advisors. Typically the bosses have strong relationship with each of their managers based on high trust. They openly share their insights, intel, and foresight with their managers on the rapidly shifting contexts their work resides in. They take individuals and the team into their confidence, so each team member and the whole team know how the leader feels on important matters. Many of these teams are perceived by others as tight-knit groups, sharp as tacks, and focused.

Many specialists and leaders deeper within the organization report feeling criticized in their interactions with their leadership team and not up to the mark.

Much of my work with individual leaders who present to senior leadership teams have indicated high levels of anxiety. Many leave meetings feeling as if they have been in an inquisition. My work with the individuals has been to help them shape their interactions as if they and the leaders are collegial peers. My work with leadership teams has taken a different direction. I have focused on exploring what underpins tensions and rifts between leaders and their staff, and then once discovered, expand trusted relationship dynamics within those leadership teams.

I use a systemic approach—that if staff felt a gap between them and the leadership team, it was likely that team members within the leadership team might well have a similar experience. I can assess there would be an in-group and an out-group within the team itself.

Inevitably this is accurate. My research frequently reveals a clique, an entrenched core group of team members, at times including the boss have had work histories within several organizations. These subgroups can include both men and women, and are perceived by the others as the in-group. In-group behaviors which exclude others might include:

- Colloquial greetings and humor
- Shared work confidences
- Predetermined decisions
- Social interactions

The remainder, the out-group, tend to be left to their own devices. Other pairs may well have previous work connections or subject matter expertise yet remain isolated from the central clique (Figure 2.2).

Cliques are entrenched subgroups which frequently form around social criteria such as:

- Attended the same college, or were neighbors
- Worked successfully together previously
- Shared sporting or leisure interests

The key for developing cohesion and mutual flows of feeling is to find strong criteria that are highly likely to illicit sincere participation and are:

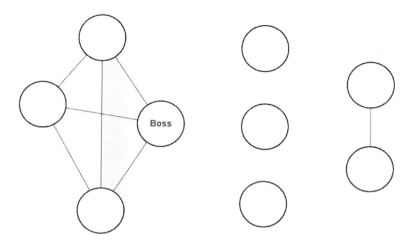

FIGURE 2.2
Clique in typical leadership team

- Relevant to the group and its stage of development
- Relevant to each individual
- Strong, enduring, and definite, and not weak, transitory, and indefinite [4]
- Solely for the purpose of expanding members' knowledge of themselves as a group

Anything less and you are working with mindless techniques and games and your people feel manipulated.

Unity and strong interpersonal work relationships are built on two or more criteria such as surviving a significant shared experience e.g., 9/11, COVID lockdowns, a challenging work project, a major health scare, loss of a family member or partner, or parenting an autistic child. Not surprisingly, people with these experiences do find one another in organizations. They find their companions. What I am talking about here is that it is the leaders' role to actively help their people find companions which will assist their work together. They do not leave building relationships and cohesion to happenstance.

Among the common criteria relevant to almost everyone are values, early family life, turning points, and leadership experiences. All four hold a rich source of shared experiences and differences in any group.

FORMING CONNECTIONS ON NEW CRITERIA

Shared experiences create bonds and a sense of shared "knowing," values, and acceptance of others. This knowing facilitates things making sense and magnifies interpersonal acceptance. Each person's sense and appreciation of the others expands. This also applies to the experiences that shaped them as a leader. Interpersonal perception expands, and each individual is perceived as far more than their job description or quirky habits.

The outcome of my work with leadership team development is typically to:

- Generate relationships to be inclusive rather than an exclusive club with inner and outer circles of influence

- Establish new ways of operating so that the leaders shift from being task-oriented leading their business groups to leading the full organization and engaging with their managers and staff
- Creating a personable, productive, results-based work culture where people are inspired to give their best

In our initial group sessions, typically I invited each person to share their experience from a number of perspectives. This may include:

- Their birth order
- A family influence on them as leaders
- A work experience that shaped them as a leader
- An unusual story of one of their ancestors

The stories flow.

These brief stories expand leaders' perceptions of one another. Appreciation of different drivers deepens. Sharing significant turning points in their lives and moments previously unknown deepens these leaders' appreciation of one another.

As we proceed, connections form around unlikely shared experiences:

- Birth order (eldest, middle, and youngest)
- Formative leadership experiences
- Unusual ancestral contributions, including stories of pioneers, innovators, stowaways, and inventors

The process of low self-disclosure has high impact. The previously entrenched clique opens up. New mutual interpersonal connections form with shared experiences and values more relevant to leading others. Understanding and acceptance of one another as trusted companions deepens. The refreshment of relationships is underway. New subgroups form including most or all group members resulting in positive mutual relationships on two criteria:

- Personal and professional respect
- Trusted confidants

No one is in an out-group based on these criteria. The vulnerability of the leaders within these groups and the shift in their culture is underway.

Colleagues perceive one another in a new light. With these expanded connections established among group members, fresh approaches to old and familiar problems can result. This is the real purpose of building connections among people.

When people have strong positive interpersonal connections, they more easily tackle the real work of the group, accessing more of their personal and professional resources.

A leader's investment in time, their hard work in choosing relevant criteria, and listening to the group's responses will result in dramatically expanded capacities for quality succinct discussions, faster decisions, and successful implementation. The result is you experience the powerful effects of expanded social cohesion in your work group.

J. L. Moreno said social cohesion occurs when the number of dyads (mutually positive pairs) is larger than one half of the group members [5]. For example, in a group of 12 people, there would be at least 7 mutually positive dyads. In the example below, everyone in the team developed positive mutual relationships (Figure 2.3). Their emotional expansiveness increased, meaning they included more people as trusted confidants. They also expanded the number of people for whom they felt care and professional respect.

Among the initial assessment interviews, I ask each person this question: *"How well are your skills, experience, and expertise used in leadership team meetings?"*

The results are frequently startling to the team. Here is an example from a typical team in which individuals rated their satisfaction five out of ten—zero being not at all and ten being "well enough." I then ask what would they want on their agenda for their satisfaction to be closer to ten. These findings can then be implemented (Figure 2.4). Unsurprisingly, the shifts tend to be from subject matter tactics to business strategy, people development, and streamlining systems and processes.

Leadership teams are able to rapidly change their agenda from tactical content problem-solving to tackling issues at the group level. This results in improved systems and processes, better people development, more strategic discussions, and a higher level of confidence in their staff's capacities as government advisors and stakeholder managers.

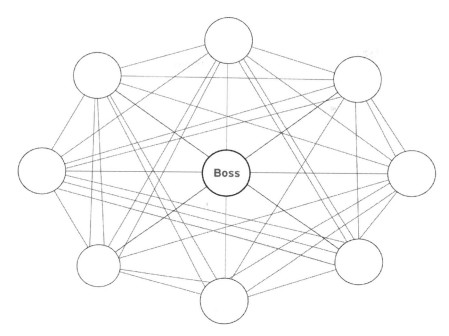

FIGURE 2.3
Typical leadership team based on high trust relationships

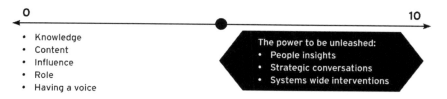

FIGURE 2.4
Leaders' satisfaction with their contributions

They become reliable trusted colleagues of one another and set up processes to ensure insights and applications with specialist briefings, instead of being *incisive critics* and *inquisitorial masters*. Leaders can draw together communities of expertise, and identify intergroup gaps and overlaps where they can capitalize their strategies. Business decisions can be concluded with implications for implementing within business units, rather than the business unit agendas dominating. Leadership team agendas shift from silo-based to a business-wide agenda (see Figure 2.5).

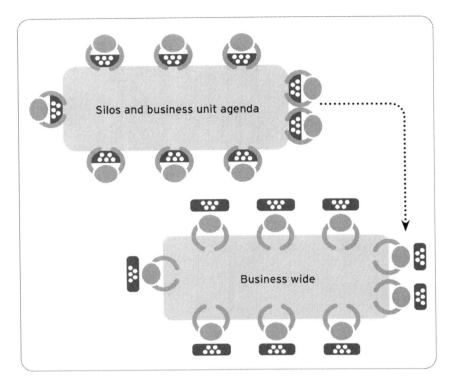

FIGURE 2.5
The team agenda shifts

FEELINGS ARE AN ORGANIZATION'S LIFE BLOOD

Leaders naively think that having a shared vision and direction is enough to unite others. Yes, shared vision and direction do go some way to igniting passions and drawing people together, but to implement a shared vision and direction requires action. Action relies on participants' responses to the leader and one another.

The nature of the relationship between the leader and those around them entirely depends on the leader's ability to draw people both to them and to one another. The *movement* toward and away from the leaders and one another is invisible, yet tangible. This movement is emotional, and described by J. L. Moreno as *tele*, a two-way flow of feeling between and among people. This flow of feeling "attracts" or "repels" individuals to one another. Tele is expressed in terms of being positive, negative, and neutral and can be described using different degrees of intensity, from weak to strong. Tele, the flow of feeling among people, increases as individuals get to know one another. People are drawn to one another or not; they are attracted or drawn to, rejected (not chosen, move away from), or not known (neutral)—the flow of feeling has an intensity from weak to strong, both projected and retrojected. Tele activates when the individuals are in proximity to one another [6].

By finding or creating shared experiences using criteria relevant to the stage of development of the group, and their agenda, leaders can build cohesion and unity. The reciprocal flows of feeling among people can be harnessed for greater productivity as people get to know one another more. Regardless of formal structures, people will privately choose to work with one another to get work done or not.

INCREASING COHESION

Using specific criteria to explore, assess, and develop relevant work relationships among group members, leaders can produce interactions that increase group cohesion by helping people discover companions— people with whom they want to work.

I continue to be intrigued by the exquisite stories revealed among group members with simple criteria. These range from the previously unspoken early death of siblings to growing up in dysfunctional families to inspired mentors and heartfelt migrant arrival experiences.

In the formation of a Federal education agency, the CEO wanted to know how many in his leadership team had experienced others joining their family growing up, as had happened to him. Astonishingly 9 of the 13 people in the group had this experience or had themselves grown up in families other than their original one. They reflected how as executives and as an agency, they found it easy to form partnerships with their new programs. Their challenge was to be recognized in their formal leadership roles by the leaders in their partner agencies. That became one focus of our work together.

This is the task of leaders—to actively mine for shared experiences and values among their people. Refreshing relationships in workgroups expands inclusion, creates fresh bases for interpersonal connections. This releases:

- New capacities
- Increased trust
- Creativity and innovation
- Cohesive communication
- Group cohesion
- Faster decisions
- Greater confidence and authenticity in interactions

If this is possible, why is it so easy for leaders to alienate their staff?

TO ALIENATE AND EXCLUDE IS TOO EASY

The childhood chant, *Sticks and stones may break my bones but names can never harm me*, is a lie. This 1862 saying is logical but inaccurate. The origin was to encourage the bullied to do what was right despite taunts from companions. In reality, leaders name-calling of staff hurts the recipients, and damages the leaders' reputation, if they have one.

The main effect of mockery, insults, and belittling is to alienate. When leaders use this as an interpersonal tool, they intend four things:

- To create distance by pushing the accused out of their inner circle of trusted companions
- To encourage subgroups or gangs of like minds to form around themselves as leader
- To demonstrate their superior powers
- To highlight the insignificance of the other

Being insulted can hurt the recipient. This hurt and subsequent fear of the behavior being repeated goes a long way to explain why those who are belittled and bullied rarely push back. The scorpion's sting is more memorable to recipients than charm offensives. Exclusion and alienation is exaggerated with an authority relationship, where one player has structural, economic, or political power over the other.

Insults and belittling belong to the category of defensive behaviors. These behaviors create distance from the defender. Defensive behaviors create an invisible yet palpable wall between themselves and the recipients.

EIGHT BEHAVIORS DEFENSIVE LEADERS OVERUSE

Whether intentional or not, persistent defensive behaviors damage relationships by forcing a distance between the defender and the other. Trust is less evident. People work together because structurally they must.

These leaders contribute value to their organizations through their knowledge and expertise, yet they engage in these unhelpful behaviors:

- **Acquiesce, walk away, or go silent in intense interactions.** Here the protagonist stops engaging and moves away physically, socially, or psychologically. The recipient can only guess what caused the other to cut off contact.
- **Justify and explain.** Leaders who "explain" in their attempt to gain understanding have the opposite effect. Listeners feel shut out. They don't want an explanation. They want to know the implications for them, their business unit, and for achieving business results. While the leader is attempting to be thoughtful and helpful, explaining or describing rarely is.
- **Make excuses.** Need I say more? We all have reasons why we act. Rarely do our reasons stack up.
- **Attack an idea or person.** Attack as the best form of defense may work in sports, but attacking a person or their idea is unhelpful in work relationships. "You are wrong" is a relationship killer in anyone's language.
- **Blame.** Blame is the opposite of taking responsibility. Naturally, there are a myriad of reasons why something fails. Hearing about that aspect is rarely interesting. Leaders who focus on discovering the root cause know that the basis of responsibility and organization learning begin by fixing what's not working and identifying how to avoid failure in the future.

- **Condemn or judge.** This defensive behavior assumes the leader is superior to whomever they are condemning or judging. They have rejected the other as not being up to their own, or to some imaginary standard.
- **Deride, are sarcastic, and/or use cynicism.** Under the guise of opinion and humor, cynicism and derision about a third party are painful to the recipient and can trap naïve listeners into being part of a gang that rejects the recipient.
- **Deny, are deluded, or lie.** These three behaviors break trust and require the moral fortitude of staff, peers, and bosses to counteract.

Leaders who use any of these behaviors with stakeholders, bosses, peers, colleagues, and staff tend to push people away. They block interactions and close others out.

RESPONSIVE BEHAVIORS BUILD RELATIONSHIPS

Leaders have access to at least seven behaviors to build relationships. These behaviors tend to attract people and draw them closer. They are classical leadership behaviors:

- Take responsibility.
- Relate to the future with vision, direction, goals, and expectations.
- Be accountable. Successful leaders are accountable for results, regardless of the outcome. They take action and respond if the desired result isn't achieved.
- Take action.
- Problem-solve and resolve issues.
- Be willing to admit mistakes: "I was wrong, my part in it was … ."
- Be unafraid to make mistakes and correct them.
- Have specific ways to add value to help others succeed.

WHY PEOPLE REJECT YOU AND WHAT YOU CAN DO ABOUT IT

Sociometric relationship language is powerful. These words describe precisely what is meant.

- **Attract**: *draw towards*
- **Reject**: *to repel, meaning not chosen on specific criteria, or to move away from*
- **Neutral**: *not known*

As a leader, it's not only possible to shape the flow of feeling you bring to any group but also essential that you do. Defensive leaders tend to have negative flows of feeling toward others. Responsive leaders tend to have positive flows of feeling toward others. The approach you take is your choice.

> Nick was quiet and tentative in his approach to his leadership team. Several team members were older than he was, and brought considerable technical expertise to the group that Nick didn't have.
>
> Nick let his experts dominate group decisions. He read the flow of feeling from his group toward him as negative, rejecting him as leader. Nick let his low self-confidence dominate what he brought to his team. I asked Nick to reverse roles with one team member who would let Nick know what he noticed. His assessment of himself: *Low energy, not interested in us, and not sure what he wants.*
>
> Nick was astonished. He tried approaching his group differently. He smiled and looked at participants as he came toward the meeting table. *"Hello everyone, great to see you all here. I'm looking forward to us nailing this legacy problem we have in front of us."*
>
> Nick himself thought he was completely over-the-top. His peer participants experienced him as positive, upbeat, and directive. Nick experienced the power of letting his real and positive feeling flow toward his group. He reported his team meetings have changed significantly.

FEELING REJECTED IS A POWERFUL EMOTION

Being rejected can be a powerful and memorable experience.

One of the downsides of professional sports, job interviews, and political elections is that there can only be one winner. These contexts are competitive—implying the candidates are a match fit—the best in the business, with experiences and capabilities fit for purpose. Pit two or more exceptional candidates for any position, sport, political elections, or job interviews—there is still only one winner.

Too often, not being the winner, or not being chosen for a job you really want, feels like rejection. But is it? With job interviews specifically, is choosing one person over another really a rejection of the one not appointed? I don't think so. My view is the real and deciding criteria only become clear after interviewing the candidates. The feeling of disappointment and losing out may feel like being rejected, but actually what is not known are the criteria which influenced the choice of the winner.

Frequently, the tele relationships among interviewers and candidates are positive. Candidates then interpret their personal disappointment as rejection by the decision-makers. That is not an accurate assessment and it's unhelpful. Leaders who act on their feelings push their thinking and wise action into the background. Questioning the process isn't going to win anyone accolade—in that you cast doubt and lack of trust on the people whose role it is to ensure the best candidate is chosen: the board, or CEO. If you so easily reject the inteviewers' decision, would you have thrived in the position?

Missing out on something about which you care deeply can be painful. How you handle the loss shapes how you will move forward from the setback. Will you enhance your reputation with this setback and build your reputation for your next success? Or will you sulk, confirming you weren't a good fit for the role.

SEVEN REASONS WHY PEOPLE REJECT YOU

People will reject leaders or choose not to work with them unless they have to, if they show these behaviors:

1. Let their self-interest dominate
2. Give no indication they value others
3. Overuse any of the nine defensive behaviors listed on page 33–34
4. Fail to recognize and/or acknowledge the contributions of others
5. Are unclear about what they want and how others can help
6. Are obsequious
7. Are clinical and logical versus being genuinely interested in people

WHAT CAN YOU DO ABOUT THIS?

Leaders, you have a choice. You can:

- Alienate or unite people
- Be invisible or be accountable
- Be rejected or be respected
- Exclude or include people
- Lead through obligation or through inspiration
- Manipulate the agenda or read the mood of your team
- Be an exclusionist or be an ally

In addition to creating positive futures for your company, customers, and people, three simple principles help leaders who want to work well with others:

- **Curiosity.** Be curious, inquire, and be prepared to listen to responses. Add phrases like *How would that work? What is your best idea? What do you think?* to requests and statements.
- **Discovery.** Learn how to help your people succeed and take those actions.
- **Appreciation.** Practice appreciation. Look people in the eye; say their name, and let them know the positive contribution you see they make.

Creating unity among diverse views is the leader's bailiwick. Creating unity means mining for shared experiences, values, and passions aligned to the vision. These in turn help people find their work companions, people they want to work with, not only the ones they have to because of the organization structure they are in. As people get to know one another beyond their names or job description, some real process from within one's life corresponds to some real process in another person's life. This generates a flow of feeling of "knowing" the other which may be positive, negative, or neutral, and creates a sense of understanding and acceptance of the self and other. You will recognize the moments when you have just met someone and yet sense you have known them for a long time and would, and do work easily with them. With others, no amount of working together strengthens your capacities to interact successfully.

CONCLUSION

Cohesion and unity in groups is created by positive interpersonal relationships based on shared values and experiences. The leader's mandate is to find creative ways to release the positive flow of feeling among group members. Leader's self-insight is the source of knowing what they can do that draw people to them, and what they do that causes people to move away from them. Chapter 3 reveals the real measure of relationships.

REFERENCES

1. A. E. Hale, *Conducting Clinical Sociometric Explorations: A Manual for Psychodramatists and Sociometrists*, Roanoke, Virginia: Royal Publishing Company, 1981.
2. J. Harter, "Employee engagement on the rise in the U.S.," 26 August 2018. [Online]. Available: https://news.gallup.com/poll/241649/employee-engagement-rise.aspx.
3. B. Tuckman, "Developmental sequence in small groups," *Psychological Bulletin*, 63(6), pp. 384–399, 1965.
4. J. Moreno, "Who shall survive?," in *Who Shall Survive?*, McLean, Virginia, American Society of Group Psychotherapy and Psychodrama, 1993, p. 99
5. J. Moreno, "Who shall survive?," in *Who Shall Survive?*, McLean, Virginia, American Society of Group Psychotherapy and Psychodrama, 1993, p186.
6. J. Moreno, *Who Shall Survive?*, McLean, Virginia: American Society of Group Psychotherapy and Psychodrama, 1993. p 26.

3

The Profound Value of Movement and Distance for Leaders

We all know leaders who use their gut feelings as a measure of concern or success. The problem is this is not an effective way to measure collaboration or engagement. A simple new concept and language for assessing productive business relationships can help fill a long-standing gap.

This is critical for effectively leading groups. Let's say you're new to your role. Your charter and your intention as leader are clear. How do you align with a group who is suspicious of you, and doesn't want to work the way you do? How do leaders implement their vision and gain alignment?

In April 2019, my partner and I spent seven days in Havana, Cuba. Our accommodation was a casa particular, a first-floor spacious family home replete with ornate first-floor balcony, overlooking the former glorious baroque apartments in Calle Neptuno. With the city in crumbling disrepair, our view was of apartments in ruins with electrical wiring haphazardly clipped to metal protuberances like unformed birds' nests.

We had the third guest room, simply furnished with terracotta painted walls and an exquisitely tiled en suite bathroom. While Havana's ambience reeks with vibrant history, there are few domestic luxuries in today's economic environment. The one luxury we had was a hairdryer in its original box proudly stored in the wardrobe.

There were two plugs in the bathroom, one labeled *international*. Naturally I plugged the hairdryer in there. After all, I am "international." Boom. The dryer flashed. Dark gray smoke poured out along with the stench of burned electronics. I leaped back. Wrong socket and no adapter.

DOI: 10.4324/9781003167334-3

Something similar happens with groups. Leaders need to be the adapter and use the right socket at the right amperage to tap into the capabilities and experience of their people.

This chapter focuses on measuring relationships, which provide the glue and ensure the right work gets done. *Distance* is the relevant measure to assess all types of relationships: interpersonal, intergroup, and stakeholder relationships. This assessment is subjective yet unnervingly accurate. Leaders use their insight and intuition, together with objective data, to assess the efficacy of any relationship.

If we think in terms of a global positioning system (GPS), the leader's relationship GPS has two specific functions:

- To accurately assess the distance between themselves and those they are leading in relation to the desired result
- To provide the tools to generate movement in precisely the right directions

NAVIGATING THE COMPLEXITY OF MULTI-FORCE STAKEHOLDER DYNAMICS

Dreams, vision, roles, mission, direction, values, and priorities all are part of the leader's toolbox—as are trust, insight, foresight, empathy, along with strategy, plans, systems, process, and action. What is often missing is the glue that might possibly draw these seething masses of elements into coherence.

Executive pay rewards movement in share price but doesn't result in inspiring organizations where people love to work to produce results for their customers. Nor does movement in share price overtly reflect the quality of the working relationship between boards and owners and boards and CEOs. New Zealand construction company Mainzeal's board operated the company in technical insolvency for seven years. It appears there was a gap between board members and their foreign owners that left board requests and their questions unanswered.

Former Thanos CEO Elizabeth Holmes was indicted for fraud because her company—once worth billions—while founded on good ideas, appears to have been run by lies and deceit. Holmes and her board were too close to one another, and the staff too distant from both to accurately assess the real picture.

Too often, leaders lose sight of their vision and strategy and are let down by their behavior with the very people they lead.

Their focus on solving problems among divisions, rather than inspiring the same people to work well together, or to ensure their relationship with their chair and board serves the organization.

CEOs need to be effectively governed. By sensing the distance between the chair and themselves, CEOs can rapidly assess whether they're isolated from the board or too close and vice versa. They could be at too great a distance for the board to trust their decisions, or too close to their chair to make effective decisions. Conversely, competent board chairs continually assess and adjust this distance according to the development of the CEO and the organization. For either side to ignore distance as a success measure on the criteria of trust and alignment in the Chair-CEO relationship would be abdicate responsibility in ensuring efficacy and role clarity.

CHAMPIONING SUBJECTIVE MEASURES

Tele relationships can be measured on two subjective continuums at any point in time:

- The strength of a trust relationship is measured from weak to strong
- Alignment can be subjectively measured with distance, using close or distant, relevant to the importance of the relationship

  Figure 3.1 provides an immediate and flexible tool that CEOs and Boards can use to assess efficacy and role clarity in their relationships. By using their perception and insight, leaders and board members can either collectively or individually make assessments of the current status of their relationships and develop strategy and actions to reset to maximize their impact. Anything less than both CEO and Chair being in the top right quadrant with a strong trusted relationship and close alignment requires action. Action requires movement within the relationship.

Longevity in the CEO and chairman's role is hugely advantageous to organizations for effective governance. This enables the relationship to

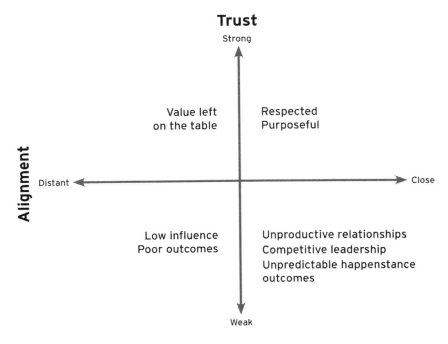

FIGURE 3.1
Subjective efficacy measures in board and CEO relationships

develop as both players grapple with organization dilemmas, shifts in strategy, and the inevitable crises.

Conventional wisdom extols the need for leadership development. Millions are invested to teach leaders strategy, decision-making, innovation, and how to harness the power of social media. Yet many leaders can't, don't, or won't have productive relationships with those whose actions influence. Many simply don't know how to build effective relationships with the groups they lead. They overvalue logic and technical data to convince others of the reasons for a decision and yet fail to use the very capacities for which they were likely appointed—their experience, intuition, and wisdom.

It's time that leaders master the basics of being inspirational:

- Know what behaviors create emotional closeness and distance with individuals and groups
- Work well with conflicting views

- Read and know how to shift the emotional tone within their organizations
- Ensure their every interaction with groups is productive

Do this and your decisions and their implementation will be people-centered and informed beyond just facts. Leaders you can influence your relationships through knowing where you stand in relation to key others relative to the business outcomes you seek. This is key for you to produce the results you want.

THE DOWNSIDE OF EMPATHY—TOO CLOSE FOR COMFORT

When I work with senior executives, I help them dramatically expand their abilities to be influential. The behaviors which help form rapid trusted working relationships rely on simple interactions from the leader's authentic self in here-and-now situations.

A frequent glitch in leaders' presence is that they want to be closer to their staff, peers, or bosses—and, as a result, they become too close. In short, they overempathize. They're so in-tune with what others want and feel that they overlook their own vision, direction, and what they want. They act as if they are Florence Nightingale, wanting to take care of everyone and everything except what's important to them.

Wanting to please others in order to move "close" is an approach that doesn't work. The leader's vision, direction, priorities, and expectations are absent. These leaders become adept at reading what their boss or staff want and do their best to meet expectations. They're adept at listening to their staff and understanding what their staff want, yet they fail to produce anything more than having an aligned staff heading in their own direction—or, worse still—repeating what they have always done to everyone's dissatisfaction. They know what their customers and stakeholders want and deliver this but overlook their own organization's mandate. These leaders overuse consultation to access others' views, then let those views dominate rather than making their own decisions by taking their own views into account.

DANGER TERRITORY: WHEN THE CHASM EMERGES, AND THE LIFELINES ARE DOWN

Hidden within group dissatisfaction are gems. Leaders often detect their group's undercurrents yet aren't able to put their finger on what's really at the heart of the matter. They know there's dissent, that there are dissatisfactions. It takes a bold leader to act. What are some of the options?

Every leader has access to two central group processes for meetings and discussions—leader-led, or group-centered leadership.

LEADER-LED

This is the most commonly used approach in organizations. Leaders decide the agenda, the purpose, and the focus of the discussion. When relationships work well, the purpose and vision are clear and shared, group cohesion is established, and results are produced.

This approach is rarely successful when there is dissent within the group. The emphasis falls on the power aspect of relationships. The leader is perceived as dominant, and in control. Speaking "truth to power" emerges where staff dare to say what is on their minds, which does not always happen when needed.

Power relationships force staff to bridge the gap. It's the staff that gathers the courage to move toward a leader when they perceive a lack of empathy from that individual. Leaders react by retreating and moving away creating a greater distance. Subgroups draw battle lines into "Us," the offended, versus "Them," the offenders. The belief that leaders won't, don't, or can't listen dominates and is frequently accurate. The #Metoo and BlackLivesMatter movements were born in this environment. The staff was astonished that their leaders couldn't or wouldn't see the problems, let alone address them. Boards of directors came too close to their offending executives. Senior executives closed ranks. Union-management negotiations frequently fall into this realm. Entrenched lines are drawn.

GROUP-CENTERED LEADERSHIP

Wilfred Bion discovered that groups work on at least two levels at any one time: the conscious, rational, task-oriented level and the more primitive emotional level. He called the former the *work group* and the latter *basic assumption (BA) groups*.[1] The work group functions well, and at other times emotional needs of group members will take over.

The work group focuses on the work at hand; the basic assumption group act as if they are together for another purpose. Those in the second group assume they're together for friendship, safety, romance, rebellion, gossip, or perhaps for devious means—and that's what they enact. Bion's work identified that this type of group has its own agenda, and it's the leader's function to assist that agenda to emerge.

Bion's research identified that when a group is in a basic assumption mode, a majority of people in the group may rely on a feeling that results in their behaving *as if* certain conditions are evident. These basic assumptions relate to primitive instincts, governed by the amygdala, whose function has been to help us survive. Naturally, these instincts are still with us. They're automatic and unconscious. When they emerge, they cause groups to split and subgroups emerge. As a result, emotionally driven behaviors dominate.

Early in my work with groups, I was amazed about what people revealed in group-centered sessions. The move from seemingly simple social niceties to in-depth authentic expression was swift and dramatic.

The main work as group members is not to "fix" the protagonists, but to connect with their human experience. Protagonists who share authentically frequently feel isolated. Their mindset is often that they're the only ones with this experience. They don't know where they stand. They fear they will be rejected, which is a valid risk for any authentic informal leader.

In some cases, the protagonist may be a lone voice. One of the revelations of #Metoo was that many others who could accompany the "lone" voices had been silenced by legal non-disclosure agreements (NDAs) facilitated by boards, executives, and HR departments. There was a systematic move to silence the complainants. Only recently with the help of journalists and social media has it been possible to discover who else might have been affected.

Knowing others who are alongside you in dramatic moments has a therapeutic effect. The relationship is repaired. You know where you stand. You see the common ground and realize you are not the only one experiencing this. As a result, you come out of isolation and know you are part of the human race.

Basic assumption social responses early in the COVID-19 pandemic saw some people panic buying with lockdowns looming, while others championed conspiracy theories. Logic and rationale failed to allay fears. Conversely, innovations resulted and, with many fearful of being exposed to the virus at work, remote work rapidly became normalized.

LEADING GROUP-CENTERED DISCUSSIONS

Agenda-free meetings are the simplest method for leaders to help groups discuss what is important to them. Instead of a structured agenda, begin the meetings by asking, "What's top of mind?" or "What's important to you right now? Let us hear from everyone." When leaders sense there's something undiscussable lurking, and the distance between them and their staff is too wide, it's invaluable to hold sessions where the focus is on "the elephant in the room."

Antony Williams describes another process called "Lay it on the table." He has participants choose an item from their surroundings to represent their concern, then put it on the table and speak to it. The leader and participants listen without questioning. Clarifying questions may be asked. Summaries at the end of the session ensure everyone understands the concerns [2]. Make no mistake. Leading these meetings well takes courage and is hard work.

Working well with dissent, opposition, and previously hidden accusations requires the same amount of hard work.

I worked with a regional leadership team. Tensions between Jeff, the CEO, and his team were intensifying. The central complaint was Jeff's delay in signing their business development proposals. His staff complained he was mired in detail, and they were sick of unnecessary delays. They felt Jeff didn't trust them. Jeff could feel the chasm between himself and his team. Tensions were running high.

The night before our meeting, the chair of the board wrote a performance letter to the CEO, copying the leadership team members. One of the team members alerted me to this and asked how we might begin a conversation about this situation. This dramatic and diverting event provided an ideal opportunity to work with the team and boss relationships.

We were seated in a circle. I asked each executive to use their body to share their response to the chair's letter. Their reactions were immediate. Two slumped forward, heads bowed. Another stood and raised a fist. Several others sat back in the chairs, stunned. I said, "Put words to your response." The range of responses included:

- *How dare the chair include us? That's a private matter between you and the chair*
- *The chair has made a mistake*
- *I am outraged they would talk with you like this. You are our CEO*

Jeff was moved. He realized two things: his team had empathy for him, and that there would be difficult conversations ahead. The group quickly decided to write to the chair, expressing their displeasure in receiving the letter. They asked for an apology and requested the matter be dealt with confidentially between the CEO and chair, as was company policy.

We moved to the business of the meeting—the elephant(s) in the room. I invited everyone to draw or represent their image of the elephant in the room. What emerged was extraordinary. On a whiteboard, Jeff drew a herd of elephants passing a grave site. One executive created a sculpture on the table. Two others drew on flip charts. Another on a second white board. I invited the group to move from image to image describing what they saw. The tension in the group dropped dramatically. We now had our agenda. We prioritized each item, and we were down to business.

Insight: Unresolved difficulties in groups evoke strong negative feelings. Leaders frequently misread these intense feelings of frustration as negativity directed toward them. Antagonists read negative feelings from the leader who is blocking them by not wanting to clarify or listen. Mutually negative tele relationships among leaders and their staff create frustration and anxiety. Distance among the players is magnified. In the emotional turmoil, leaders see mutiny. Staff members see out-of-touch direction, little understanding of context, and poor relationships.

Anxious leaders tend to move away from their teams. This creates a chasm when what is required is for leaders to move closer to their team by providing a process—an open door for a conversation about their concerns and how they might be addressed.

Leaders can access ways to address tensions within groups. A simple open agenda session with *"What's on your mind?"* helps identify the concerns people have in their work together. Groups gain confidence when they know their concerns are heard and taken sincerely. That is the work of the group—leader included.

WHO IS IN, WHO IS OUT, AND WHY THAT MATTERS

There's a strong direct correlation between productivity and how much people feel they belong to organizations, are understood, and accepted.

Recent research from BetterUp shows that if workers feel like they belong, companies reap substantial bottom-line benefits: better job performance, lower turnover risk, and fewer sick days. High belonging was linked to a whopping 56% increase in job performance, a 50% drop in turnover risk, and a 75% reduction in sick days. For a 10,000-person company, this would result in annual savings of more than $52 million [3].

Leaders often overlook the fact that belonging is a basic human need. The desire for logic and the fear of emotional expression have created conditions better suited for automatons rather than humans. The fact that care, friendliness, and kindness don't take much time has eluded many leaders. Belonging creates closeness to the organization, work group, vision, clients, or sector.

Social connections are just as important in workplaces, and yet a *Harvard Business Review* 2019 report in US organizations found that 40% of people say that they feel isolated at work [4].

This is an astonishing and unnerving finding. How can this be?

J. L. Moreno identified the *social atom* as a basic structure for all humans. It's the smallest number of people you need to keep learning and be socially alive. Your original social atom is the group of early caregivers and siblings. As you grow older, your social atom includes relatives, friends, neighbors, pets, and important people who may have died. Their interrelationships with you and the others in your social atom make up the cultural atom which holds the family values enacted in your behaviors and counter-behaviors. In dysfunctional families, many things go wrong like carer-to-child neglect, abuse, or abandonment. In essence, when the caregiver is physically and/or emotionally distant from the child, or in response to tragedies like school shootings, or unexpected deaths of family members, the child learns coping behaviors.

An adult's sense of belonging and of being understood, liked, and accepted has its genesis in early family life and greatly influences how they will behave in everyday relationships and groups.

As adults, an individual's behavior benefits from social atom repair, either immediately or later in life. Unsurprisingly, organizational dynamics such as a loved manager leaving or upheavals from restructures frequently and unintentionally replicate the early family experiences of abandonment and loss of important others. The repair is frequently a trusted caring relationship with an adult that evokes new behaviors through encouragement, companionship, therapy, and learning. In organizational life, trusted caring relationships may be with bosses, peers, friends, partners, coaches, or mentors.

Collaboration, and cooperation do not make sense to anyone when personal safety and emotional survival are at stake. The social isolation and lack of companionship during interpersonal or team conflicts, restructures, mergers, and acquisitions are a large part of the painful organization experience. No one sees what's happening and no one comes to help.

The development of any successful leader's professional identity includes the capacity to continually build and rebuild their social atom to include trusted companions, including in any moment.

Sweet and Shook in Accenture's 2020 study, *Getting to Equal 2020: The Hidden Value of Culture Makers,* found two-thirds of leaders they surveyed (68%) feel they create empowering environments—in which employees can be themselves, raise concerns, and innovate without fear of failure—but just one-third (36%) of employees agreed with this assessment [5].

This alarming gap dramatically affects profitability and productivity. Turning this around lies in the hands of leaders, or, more accurately, in their mindset and their language. There is much to do.

According to *Harvard Business Review,* US businesses spend nearly $8 billion each year on diversity and inclusion (D&I) trainings that miss the mark because they neglect the individual's need to feel included [4].

Why is it we are prepared to invest in teaching concepts, listing facts, and giving information, yet we neglect measuring the results to see how well this learning is applied?

HOW DO WE INCLUDE OR EXCLUDE?

Leaders who *include* others are more likely to:

- Look people in the eye when they speak to them
- Greet people in their first language
- Know people's names
- Know the results of what they do
- Introduce them to others

Leaders who *exclude* others are more likely to:

- Use passive language and collective pronouns
- Look anywhere but at people
- Favor specific individuals or subgroups over others

Let me be clear. A leader's ability to make personal choices is an essential ingredient for successful relationships, as is the ability to say no. These are the tools with which leaders can create emotional closeness and distance relevant to what they want to achieve.

What doesn't work (consciously or unconsciously):

- Overlooking or acting as if individuals or groups on a specific social criterion don't exist
- Assuming individuals and specific groups don't have relevant skills or experience
- Excluding specific individuals or groups from your organization based on social criteria—and not actively attracting or recruiting them

IT'S TOO EASY TO EXCLUDE

The cumulative effect of long-time personal and institutional exclusion results in sensitivity to many behaviors. People are excluded by leaders when they are:

- Dropped from the formal or informal email lists.
- Not invited to discussions or meetings.

- Not acknowledged as report writers or contributors.
- Not welcomed to new settings.
- Held back by outdated legislative exclusions or requirements, such as land ownership requirements, focus on binary sexual identity, or racial persecution. For example, few Aboriginals in Western Australia had driver's licenses, as most indigenous people didn't have official birth certificates—a requirement for a driver's license; women didn't want to register their baby's birth being fearful of their baby being taken away [6], young aboriginal people can be refused bail as they may not have a stable address, they prefer to move around.
- Give more weight to the opinions of people who are most like them in demographics.
- Only use one way of getting input from employees, i.e., expecting people to speak up at a brainstorming session when many people aren't comfortable just speaking out or do better by writing ideas or in a small group discussion.
- Offer a general invite to events. People who are not in the dominant culture, especially if there are a small number, assume they are not really included in the invite.

Leaders actively exclude when they:

- Use limited personal pronouns
- Assume masculine pronouns to include everyone
- Use stereotypes, e.g., Black Americans are likely to cause trouble
- Ignore or be ignorant of indigenous language and group behavior
- Enact zealous suspicions of specific racial groups
- Use outdated rules of behavior
- Don't sanction those who favor one particular racial or binary sexual identity group over others
- Interrupt and talk over people who have English as second language
- Say they don't look at people as different from them (not the same as eye contact versus no eye contact) but use body language to exclude

Each of these behaviors creates an emotional distance among the excluded individuals and the leaders and institutions enacting these behaviors. Some leaders I meet don't see themselves as separate from the group they are in—they are with "their people." To be an individual is an alien concept to them. This contrasts directly with my work with other leaders, which is to assist them to relate well within the groups they influence. Their development as leaders is to accept that they are an integral part of the groups they lead.

MINDSET AND LANGUAGE

Mindset and language are two of the power tools of a successful leader.

Like Bion, Edgar Shein noticed that groups would form for purposes other than the immediate task at hand. Shein found that an individual brings multiple other group identities into any work group—influences from family, occupations, neighborhood, friendships, prior employers, cultural experiences, and more—and that they experience new situations with anxiety. This anxiety is there before new configurations, new identities, and new associations are built. He noted three main interpersonal needs operate as mindsets to connect with others:

- Inclusion or identity—*Who can I be in this group?*
- Control, influence, and power—*How much will I be able to influence here?*
- Acceptance and intimacy—*Will I be liked and accepted here?* [6]

My observations and experience concur with Schein's, and this has been the basis of much of my work with leaders and organizations. When leaders fail to consciously attend to basic human needs in their groups, anxiety rises, and the group is thrown off its purpose. Conversely, when these needs are considered, anxiety reduces dramatically and positive feelings flow among participants result. The group task becomes central.

EVERY WORD MATTERS

Active language enables leaders to create personalized immediacy and accountability, which will draw in others: *I want to talk with you about our approach to this current crisis, so each of you knows your role, and what success will look like.*

Passive language lacks personal accountability. Listeners may remain neutral with no movement forward: *We have decided on our approach. The team will know what to do and how to measure success.*

Cori Bush is a single mom, a nurse, a former COVID patient, and the first Black woman from Missouri to be elected to the US Congress. In her victory speech on election night in November 2020, she openly identified with many groups who had been marginalized and excluded by government and by "mainstream" society. She spoke directly to these individuals and groups. She'd stood in their shoes and looked at the world through their eyes, and that became clear as she masterfully included them in her remarks:

> *I was running ... I was that person running for my life across a parking lot, running from an abuser. I remember hearing bullets whizz past my head and at that moment I wondered: "How do I make it out of this life?"*
>
> *I was uninsured. I've been that uninsured person, hoping my healthcare provider wouldn't embarrass me by asking me if I had insurance. I wondered: "How will I bear it?"*
>
> *I was a single parent. I've been that single parent struggling paycheck to paycheck, sitting outside the payday loan office, wondering "How much more will I have to sacrifice?"*
>
> *I was that COVID patient. I've been that COVID patient gasping for breath, wondering, "How long will it be until I can breathe freely again?"*
>
> *I'm still that same person. I'm proud to stand before you today knowing it was this person, with these experiences, that moved the voters of St Louis to do something historic. St Louis: my city, my home, my community. We have been surviving and grinding and just scraping by for so long, and now this is our moment to finally, finally start living and growing and thriving. So, as the first Black woman, nurse, and single mother to have the honor to represent Missouri in the United States Congress, let me just say this. To the Black women. The Black girls. The nurses. The single mothers. The essential workers. This. Is. OUR. Moment. [7]*

The mindset and words of leaders can either unite people or alienate them. They can include people or exclude them. Cory Bush with her deep self-disclosure clearly put herself into the group of politicians who unite and include people. Her speech draws people in. She brings previously disenfranchised groups closer and enables them to feel part of society—rather than to feel separate, left out, and isolated.

REFERENCES

1. W. R. Bion, *Experiences in Groups*, Sussex: Tavistock, 1959.
2. A. Williams, *OUR House: Visual and active consulting*, Second Edition, NY 10017: Routledge, 2020.
3. BetterUp, "The value of belonging at work: new frontiers for inclusion," BetterUp, 2021 and Beyond.
4. E. W. Carr, A. Reece, G. Rosen Kellerman and A. Robichaux, "The value of belonging at work," *Harvard Business Review*, no. December, 2019.
5. Sweet and Shook, "Getting to equal 2020, the hidden value of culture makers," Accenture.
6. E. D. Schein, *Organization Culture and Leadership: A Dynamic View.*, San Francisco: Jossey-Bass, 1986.
7. C. Bush, Writer, *This is Our Moment*. [Performance]. Theguardian.com/us-news/video, November 2020.

4

Reading People Not Content

In 2017, the Weinstein Company fired CEO and cofounder Harvey Weinstein after more than 100 women came forward with claims of sexual harassment. This was not long after Roger Ailes, former head of Fox News, left the network after being accused of similar behavior. In both cases, the companies involved paid millions of dollars in hush money to survivors of their CEOs' bad behavior.

How do these situations happen? It's human nature to try and explain away or ignore behavioral evidence that doesn't have an immediate negative impact on tangible results. We lose confidence to remove people who are obstacles, because we imagine we don't really know what happened, or we're not willing to call out the behavior. We fear being derided, or called a hypocrite, or that the behavior is denied. Decisions are made that reflect care and protection of leaders over staff.

Too often, we are blinded by our own feelings, rather than seeing the light right in front of us. In this chapter, we examine a fresh source of data: reading people, rather than relying on logic or content. Solutions that take multiple stakeholder perspectives into account can be easily accessed.

With over 15 years of working with experienced and emerging leaders, I've been struck by three things:

- Their depth of knowledge of specific content
- The vast experiences, both personal and professional, many of them bring to their work
- Their preparation for meetings based on delivering their content

Trying to have others understand what should be done by sharing your knowledge and information alone is not enough to move people into

DOI: 10.4324/9781003167334-4

55

alignment. A leader's ability to "read" and respond to the emotional drivers of key stakeholders is at the heart of alignment and change.

NAVIGATING THE RIGHT RELATIONSHIPS WITH MULTIPLE STAKEHOLDERS

In the past, leaders have very deliberately read and measured a set of criteria. Unfortunately, those were the wrong things to be tracking. Even a balanced scorecard rarely includes measures to indicate how well leaders are leading. While financial data, engagement measures, and key performance indicators (KPIs) give indications of organization success, they don't tell the whole story.

> *If we measure the wrong thing, we will do the wrong thing. If our measures tell us everything is fine when they really aren't, we won't make the right decisions* [1].

Joseph Stiglitz

What should we measure to ensure we are appropriately leading people? Closely tied to measuring distance and closeness in relationships (from Chapter 3) is another essential measure—the capacity to "read" people. When this capacity is absent or overlooked, dramatic failures result. Two examples follow: one in New Zealand and the other in France and Japan.

In 2019, after the ANZ (Australia New Zealand) bank in New Zealand posted a $2 billion dollar profit, the CEO of nine years suddenly left.

In 2018–2019, there'd been a widely publicized review of Australian financial institutions to identify deficiencies and complacency in culture and corporate governance. While the CEO's tenure was considered profitable, it appeared that his benefits, set up a decade earlier, were dramatically in excess of those for executives in allied sectors. This did not reflect well on the bank in the current austere climate. The result was a dramatic end to a previously highly successful career. Why couldn't this CEO have been more alert to this shift in perception?

At about the same time, a sudden, dramatic gap emerged between Carlos Ghosn, former chairman of Nissan in Japan and Renault in France, and his bosses. For years, Ghosn has been revered for his leadership, innovations, and accomplishments. But in 2019, when Nissan rejected Ghosn, his French counterparts remained publicly silent. Ghosn was jailed in Japan, and then stunningly escaped to Lebanon.

Ghosn had misread his bosses, colleagues, and staff. He believed they continued to go along with the direction and actions he was taking with the companies he led, or that he could bring them around to his point of view. But the truth was they saw what he was doing was illegal. They no longer supported him and stepped back from him.

The gaps between Ghosn and his bosses, his peers, and staff widened. He badly misread where he stood with each.

MIND THE GAP

To an astute observer, three likely relationship misreads can be immediately seen in both cases.

1. First, there were likely gaps between these two CEOs and their respective board chairs. The efficacy of the CEO-Board relationship is a crucial measure impacting any CEO. Being able to read the shifts in distance and closeness and the strength of the relationship relative to their functions and immediate context is critical to CEO success. Being frank, forthright, and authentic is also essential for a chair to effectively govern a CEO. In both cases, this was either lost or avoided.

   While infrequently "read," the perceived gaps between governance and the CEOs in these two examples are a precise indicator that all was not well, and the matter needed to be addressed rapidly. The tele relationship between the CEOs, their governance structures, and their peers had weakened trust, and the distance among the key players had expanded. Both CEOs failed to "read" this.

2. Both CEOs' reading of public opinion and their own investors was misaligned. In Australia, bank surpluses are not something the public expects or celebrates. Investors do. Yet both the public and investors have their interests focused on wise use of funds—particularly their own. Social responsibility and ethical behavior are important. When the public and investors are under pressure financially, they won't tolerate perceived self-indulgences and a culture of entitlement by company leaders. The ANZ CEO's job benefits may have been the norm for a financial institution a decade earlier, but in 2019, chauffeur-driven cars, a corporate-funded wine cellar, and below-market pricing on a multi-million dollar family home for the CEO's family were not. The culture of entitlement was over.

   In Ghosn's scenario, CEO pay and privileges were at the behest of the company governors, not the bailiwick of the CEO and his allies. Ghosn's transgressions resulted in him being charged with fraud and criminal behavior.

3. If the relationships between the CEOs and their peers had been positive, close, and mutual, both executives would likely have been alerted to the change in climate of financial governors, the public, and board opinion. They or their board chairs would have been alerted to the shift. We can assume that both CEOs had become isolated from the groups and individuals crucial to their ongoing success. They failed to understand the devastating impact of this mistake.

The perceived loss of reciprocity within their relationships and the widening gaps in these three areas contributed to unexpected and unsatisfying ends to otherwise distinguished and successful careers for both of these CEOs.

These are two prime examples of misreading the emotional drivers of key people and group relationships. The consequences of bosses overlooking drivers of antisocial behavior are dire. Informal networks of relationships and interactions influence formal decision-making structures by reflecting people's emotional drivers, rather than relying on logic or content. No amount of bottom-line success and business expertise can overcome the subtle shifts within the informal networks of relationships of who listens to whom, and who influences whom. In Chapter 5, we will explore the nature and function of informal networks of relationships in greater detail.

Reading and responding to distance and closeness among leaders and their stakeholders are significant success measures, along with the capacity to read people. These are concepts of significant learning that many leaders still need to master.

At a microlevel, we have all very likely misread similar key relationships. You may have thought you were closer to friends, colleagues, or partners than they actually thought they were to you.

Here are examples of everyday versions of this experience. The gap with informal networks versus formal structures works to the leader's disadvantage:

- A close colleague poaches your best team member
- A long-time colleague doesn't let you know they have the private information that your CEO is requesting from you
- Your close friend lets you know they're having an affair with your partner
- You realize your boss has known you are being restructured out of the organization for weeks, but has only just told you what's happening

I've experienced each of these instances—perhaps you have as well. Each time trust is broken, and feelings run high as you reassess where others stand in relation to you.

These are moments when your world is turned upside down. You become aware of yawning gaps among your knowledge, your psyche, and your heart. Trust is broken, or may never have been there at all. You have misread your relationships.

INTERPERSONAL PERCEPTION MATTERS

Understanding where others stand in relation to you is called interpersonal perception—that capacity to read others and the work being done. Leaders develop interpersonal perception through experience, guess work, testing, curiosity, and intuition. This type of learning is not intellectual. This learning is experiential and is a mix of insight, reflection, knowing your own values, and reading others' values through their behavior. Accurately reading how they themselves are perceived is a central capacity for successful leaders.

Steve led the insights group in a large public value corporation. His ability to confidentially develop strategy, along with his positive relationships with senior leaders, helped his group attract significant investment for developments. Steve doubted that his team was on board with the changes he had in mind. He sensed a gap with the team and thought that they felt negatively about him. He wanted to find out what was behind this. I suggested he ask each member of his team for their input while I facilitated the process. Steve took a deep breath, concerned with what he might hear, but agreed to give this a chance.

I proposed each of his team members outline three things they enjoyed about working with Steve, and one thing they wanted him to change. Each of his direct reports agreed to participate. To a person, the overwhelming development message to Steve was, *Be more personal. Be human.* Steve discovered he was perceived overwhelmingly positively, but none of his team "knew" him. This left Steve in a dilemma. He was an intensely private person, but he wanted to be closer to his team to be confident they would implement his vision. He was affected by his direct reports' courage in being so open with him.

I coached Steve to use his weekly town hall meetings to share:

- His insights of the group's progress
- How the group's progress positively impacted him and the business
- Two or three successes with the group
- A self-disclosure from his family life

Steve followed this process. He also implemented it with each of his direct reports. The response was immediate, positive, and strong. More people spoke with Steve. They let him know their difficulties and alerted him to the problems they saw within the division. They asked for his advice. The collective intelligence within his group dramatically increased. His own team shared their own insights into the business. Steve's appreciation of his direct reports strengthened dramatically. He became closer to them and they in turn became closer to him. He brought more dilemmas to them to solve. He was more tuned into their progress, rather than focusing on the many roadblocks they faced. Steve was more aware of the individuals and their talents within his wider group. His confidence in having difficult conversations increased. Steve's reputation as a personable able leader rose, along with his ability to read accurately how well his people could deliver the group's strategy.

Steve's willingness to hear how his direct reports perceived him created an opportunity for his staff to better be able to "read him." His simple self-disclosures enabled his staff to read him better and yes, he was approachable and "human."

THE SOCIOMETRIC JOLT

The experience of having people you trusted pull away or subtly distance themselves from you is called a *sociometric jolt*. People you had thought were companions reveal that's not the case.

The language to describe these experiences is dramatic:

- Back stabbing
- Gaslighting
- Being thrown under a bus
- Two-faced
- Betrayal

Experience any one of these jolts and you may question your judgment and your wisdom. Rightly so. You are about to undertake significant personal learning. Others experience burnout, where they have been giving more of themselves, without the relationship mutuality they thought was there.

In any setting, knowing the criteria upon which informal relationships are based is crucial for leaders. Rather than the formal structures, it is the informal networks of relationships which dictate what gets done and how (Chapter 5 includes a greater explanation on informal networks of relationships).

Unless a leader has built strong informal networks of relationships based on trust and inclusion, their position and acceptance in the organization are merely illusory.

Certainty in the shifts of interpersonal perception creates confidence. Leaders who can't accurately assess who is on their team end up doubting themselves.

In this chapter, I will introduce you to tools to help you better read people. I'll give you options for handling situations that will inevitably occur during your career. Building on Chapter 3, which explained how to use distance as a measure of relationships, we can now focus in greater depth on how you can move closer or create distance through reading and responding to an individual's relevant emotional drivers.

Several years ago, I was at a Social Network Analysis conference in Vancouver, British Columbia. I endured a 45-minute presentation where the presenter determinedly showed every single one of her 145 PowerPoint slides. Her mastery of the information was readily apparent. But her ability to connect with us as the audience—or her desire to do so—was non-existent. I nearly died from too much information. I couldn't wait to escape to the freedom of interacting with my peers. It was like being fed burned toast. I didn't want a taste of what she had to offer. She remained closer to her content than to us as her audience.

This is the trap that captures many specialists. They're closely tied to their content but remain far removed from the very people they want to influence.

Few business audiences expect presentations that have excessive information, too many complex diagrams, and a focus on heady concepts. Most audiences want to be confident they and their business will benefit from applying the material and that they can trust they will work well with whomsoever is presenting this to them.

READING THE EMOTIONAL TONE OF THE GROUP

The basic power tool for anyone learning how to work with groups is to learn to read and report the emotional tone of a group. I teach this to the groups with whom I work, particularly early in the process. I invite participants to assess the emotional tone of our group by guesswork. For leadership sessions where participants are first meeting one another, the typical responses I hear from the group about their mood are *uncertain, friendly, tentative,* and *anticipation.* In groups where interpersonal conflict is being addressed, typical responses are *anxious, stimulated, tense,* and *excited.*

Any leader can make these assessments by tuning into their own feelings and by assuming their own emotional responses that are at least in part related to the anticipated meeting. The leader becomes the emotional tuning fork. With practice, leaders become more adept at learning which feelings are their own and which belong to the group. Leaders should let their assessments inform how they begin the meeting/conversation/ presentation in order to get to the outcome they want to achieve.

If the leader reads the tone of the group as anxiety, they can then provide certainty by outlining their purpose and plan on how things are to proceed. This immediately increases certainty. Think of the revered anticipation when former Apple CEO Steve Jobs revealed new products. Think of the anxiety and loss of hope of workers in many food outlets and travel businesses worldwide when their bosses announced closures because of the COVID-19 pandemic. How well leaders read the emotional tone at these moments dictates their impact and choices as leaders.

Any of these moments are opportunities for leaders to decide whether and how to orient their comments to:

- Relevantly engage
- Ignore the feeling level and carry on regardless
- Inflame the feelings of anxiety, anger, or delight and euphoria

JUST WHO IS THE CUSTOMER?

Thinking the customer must be external lulls leaders into blinkered thinking. Leaders have multiple customer relationships to which they need to relate at any one time. They're involved in numerous, fluid, interconnected relationship systems. Their ability to have multiple functional relationships is essential. The immediate context dictates where to focus. These multiple relationship systems include:

1. Internal to the organization
   - Governance
   - Bosses
   - Peers and colleagues
   - Staff
2. External to the organization
   - Key stakeholders
   - Customers
   - Suppliers
   - Professional colleagues
   - Friends and family

Rethinking who is the customer enables leaders to refocus. Leaders then have choices on the outcome they want from any interaction, what they emphasize, and how they can achieve success.

Gary is a visionary vice president of a social services organization. He wanted to make significant inroads in dealing with many of his agency's failures, but he had inherited much of his staff at a time of government policy change. Gary felt they lacked capability, capacity, and experience. By employing experienced successful contract negotiators and managers from existing national authorities, he knew he could build on existing delivery relationships, halve the cost-of-service delivery, and guarantee results for his organization. I reviewed the paper he wrote for his boss and for peer endorsement. There were 20 pages of text making the case for savings and success.

Two things stood out for me:

- The case for change was lost in the dense content. The dramatic improvements to the business were hidden within the paper.
- His boss and peers would be bombarded with high-quality information, yet their wisdom, experience, and insights were not sought or used in the decision to proceed.

Gary rejected my advice and struggled to get his paper included on the leadership team agenda. The decision was deferred. An innovative opportunity was lost, and the reputation of both Gary and his agency suffered.

Gary is not alone. I've worked with hundreds of executives whose approach to leading change is profoundly visionary, intellectually logical, and based on giving people the information they need to be convinced. The former is essential. The ensuing two are satisfice.

Along with the outcome being sought, two key premises should be priorities for success:

- Your audience is your customer
- Make your audience central to your presentation, not your content

As leaders, you will radically increase your influence in your organization with these five simple steps (Figure 4.1).

FROM CHUGGING ALONG TO OVERDRIVE: PRESENTATIONS AND DECISIONS

1. **Focus on People**
   Focus your personal communication directly on the people who will influence the decision, not on how you might increase their understanding of your specialized content. Direct succinct personal language works best.

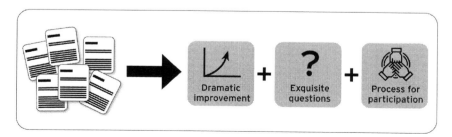

FIGURE 4.1
Shift in preparation emphasis

Most people in groups and meetings want their skills, experience, and expertise to add value, yet rarely are they invited to apply this in meetings. Unwittingly, forcing executives to take in more content puts them in a one-down position. This releases an act-hunger in them. Their unsatiated longing to influence activates haphazard contributions and questions on detail that are either competitive or aggressive in their desire to regain equality in their relationships.

2. **Purpose and Outcome Are King**

The big shift is to identify the purpose of the presentation, the outcome you want, and the outcome your audience is likely to want.

The latter, pinning the audience outcome, is the most demanding work of preparation. In Gary's example, the outcome he wanted was clear: turn the failures of social services delivery into a cost-effective, high-functioning service that dramatically improved client's lives, while building his agency's reputation. Those involved in endorsing the decision would agree. His peers on the leadership team might want the additional outcome of "increased confidence that ensuing stakeholder gaps and overlaps were addressed."

Once your purpose or outcome is clear, you'll know which three to four dramatic improvements to emphasize:
- The condition of your organization
- The condition of your customers and/or stakeholders
- Bottom-line value

3. **Express Your Appreciation**

Staff who know they are appreciated are more motivated, more productive, and go the extra mile. Leaders can ensure everyone brings their best to group interactions and decisions by their simple expression of appreciation.

Leaders' simple sincere appreciations appear as social niceties with peers and are powerful motivators. In leadership team meetings, possibilities include:
- *Each of you brings a depth of expertise and experience which helps us tackle what is in front of us*
- *I know each of you has had ideas and experience we will need to create a breakthrough on this*
- *I am confident that the talent around our table will land us up where we want to be*

4. **Craft an Exquisite Question**

   To incite the depth and quality of interaction worthy of executive decisions, pending investment, and disruption, anyone presenting or leading a conversation needs to craft exquisite questions that:
   - Tap into the expertise and experience of those present
   - Generate purposeful conversations and decisions
   - Significantly move everyone toward the outcomes being sought

   I worked on meeting protocols with a leadership team. We practiced generating exquisite questions by discussing a board meeting the previous day where several direct reports had made skillful presentations to the board about a significant change management project. Their exquisite question to one another was, "*What do we communicate to our direct reports to show we appreciate their impressive development?*"

   The subsequent contributions from each executive generated a list of ten insights and observations from their bosses. The executives also noted four actions they themselves could take to improve their game for future board meetings.

5. **Create a Process for Participation**

   Why is it so many meetings go awry? Essentially, levels of meaningful participation are low. Participants tend to replicate default survival behaviors from earlier experience of family mealtimes, their cultural settings, major life events, or their former school days. They:
   - Dominate by overtalking and overparticipating
   - Remain silent and watchful
   - Wish they were somewhere else

   It's no wonder why so many meetings don't work.

   By creating and giving simple directions and processes for participation, people can effectively collaborate using the most of their wisdom and experience. The leader's direction can be as simple as the following:

   I'll take five minutes to discuss the major business improvements and how we can navigate roadblocks. Then I want to hear from each of you. Tell us the best contribution you could make that would have the most impact on your area as we implement this initiative (Figure 4.1).

And there you have it. This is the preparation for leaders who want to have powerful interactions in group settings. For both online and in-person meetings, my best advice for presenters and meeting chairs is to use these five principles.

COLLABORATION

Use the five principles outlined above to look through the eyes of others as you hold to your own agenda, you'll shift from being seen as the *lone-ranger* to *collegial collaborator* (see Figure 4.1).

Tap into their experience and expertise with your exquisite question and provide a meaningful process for participation; people have the experience of being respected and valued. Your audience shifts from being recipients to being collaborators. You have companions working toward shared outcomes, rather than bystanders or competitors. Each holds their own agenda and works toward a shared outcome.

How does this work in practice?

> And so we lift our gazes not to what stands between us
> but what stands before us.
> We close the divide because we know, to put our future first,
> we must first put our differences aside [2].
>
> —*Amanda Gorman* (**Gorman, 2021**)

By wisely reading the depressed social and business mood, a digital marketing company, a bank, a sports stadium, a rural takeout restaurant, and an international sport game uncovered brilliance with the exquisite question, "*How do we lift people's spirits using our shared value through social purpose?*"

In late 2020, the New Zealand All Blacks rugby team played four test matches with the Australian Wallabies—pitting New Zealand and Australia's national rugby teams against each other. The second game was in Auckland. Since New Zealand had no COVID-19 community transmission, a full in-person crowd was permitted. Anticipation from players and fans was intense.

An unusual alliance developed among a marketing company, a bank, a rural takeout restaurant, and a sports stadium. Dentsu marketing company approached their client, the ASB bank, who had secured naming rights to the Auckland City Stadium. They proposed the ASB bank gift their naming rights for one week. The Stadium CEO agreed to this arrangement for the week of the game. Dentsu created a national competition for the rights, which was won by a rural fish and chip shop, Kaikoura Coopers Catch (KCC).

Kaikoura, a rural seaside New Zealand town devastated in the 2016 earthquake, had been decimated again by the dramatic decline in tourism because of COVID-19. KCC not only won a week's worth of naming rights to the stadium, but also received national publicity, and their products were sold at the game. Kaikoura was under the spotlight at a high-profile international sporting event. The power of this simple collaboration was founded on reading the emotional drivers for each group:

- Dentsu's profile as a creative marketer dramatically increased
- ASB and the Auckland Stadium expanded their reputations as generous benefactors
- The profile of Kaikoura's Coopers Catch as an attractive destination was dramatically lifted, which resulted in increased income from sales
- The generosity and feel-good factor was a relief to many in the New Zealand population, among an overload of dire political and pandemic bad news
- The overall collaboration was an inspiring experiment in social and business recovery

Long-time collaborators exist in many disciplines. Consider singer-songwriters Elton John and Bernie Taupin; basketball players Michael Jordan and Scottie Pippin, with coach Phil Jackson of the Chicago Bulls; COO Sheryl Sandburg and CEO Mark Zuckerberg of Facebook; and Amazon's Jeff Bezos and Andy Jassy [3].

Conversely, we know when collaboration *doesn't* work. The trite anacronym TEAM (Together Each Achieves More) is not always true. Multiple studies reveal 70–90% of mergers and acquisitions fail [4]. In

New Zealand, habitual public service reorganizations and "lift, shift and drop" of business units fail to deliver the desired results. This is not because of the visionary optimism of the leaders. Instead, it's the leaders' failure to read and address the reluctance of their teams. Leaders think people are reluctant to move from their embedded cultures. That's not the case. The players simply don't know who their new work colleagues really are. Interpersonal differences outweigh the business outcomes, unless new purposeful connections are made connecting people in the two entities and compelling common ground is found.

Successful leaders read the people implications of changes in context. In the early days of COVID-19, Dr Tristram Ingham [5] came up with the concept of "bubbles" while advising the Ministry of Health early on in the pandemic response for the disability sector. This concept, which limits the number of close contacts with whom any individual can reside, captured the imagination of the Prime Minister, made pragmatic sense to health officials, and most New Zealanders. With a few days' notice of the first national level 4 lockdown, people traveled home to be with those close to their hearts, their bubble. What was astonishing to any observer was that people rapidly knew who those people were.

Just as Steve Jobs and his team had done in introducing the iPhone and General Motors CEO Mary Barra slimmed down the company's ten-page dress policy to simply "Dress appropriately," Ingham and his colleagues established a powerful concept which resonated with the population. Their expertise with disrupted social structures, together with their astute reading of the New Zealand population's negative attitude to compliance, hit the jackpot with the term "bubbles." While COVID-19 raged throughout most of the world, the number of infections and deaths within New Zealand was kept extremely low as citizens stayed within their bubbles.

SYSTEM NOT LINEAR THINKING IN LEARNING TO READ PEOPLE

The main tool in leaders' toolkit is their ability to read the shifting contexts they are in. Every decision they make is based within this capacity. Unwittingly, many leaders fail to read the impacts on their peers and staff and their responses within the shifting context. They act as if they are navigating a storm without their GPS.

Four ways to up your people reading game:

1. *Listen:* Tune into what people around you are saying. This gives you immediate responses to pending decisions and alerts in roadblocks in implementing new systems or procedures and conflicts that are interfering in business progress.
2. *Be curious:* Ask questions to discover the informal responses. Ask people you know who are well connected throughout the organization. Ask people whose insights you trust: *"What's your take on how this will land?" "What's the word out on the street?"*
3. Set up a daily ten minutes culture intel session during unexpected change. Do this with your leadership team, or a group you bring together specifically for this purpose. Hear from everyone: What's our inside intel? What is our stakeholder intel?
4. Ensure you have someone in your team, or close by you, who is an astute reader of people's responses. Their role with you is to be your litmus paper for implementation.

CONCLUSION

Once you have accepted that leading is not mastery of content and knowledge but mastery of relationships, you can learn to read people. Awareness of the underlying emotional tones in groups helps leaders shape the way they lead people and run meetings. They know when and how to create stability, and when and how to empower others. They know how to commission work successfully based on identifying outcomes, and directing whether they want a completed paper, a working document, or to expect major revisions as more context is revealed. They design exquisite questions that tap into the experience and expertise of those around them. They take care in establishing a process, so it is easy for people to contribute. They assume nothing. They learn to be experts in crafting processes where their employees want to participate.

We know shared experience draws people together. This moving toward others creates another group structure which needs leaders attention—the informal networks of relationships. I have alluded to this group phenomenon several times. Chapter 5 goes into greater depth on the value of getting to know the impact of informal networks of relationships, how to make links to the formal decision structures, and learning how to generate new networks of relationships within your organization.

NOTES

1. Joseph Stiglitz, Nobel laureate in economics; long-time influential champion for large-scale reform of economic systems.
2. Gorman, Amanda, Former US Youth Poet Laureate. *The hill we climb*. Presidential Inauguration 20 January 2021.
3. Bezos and Jassy's 24-year relationship culminated in Jassy recently being named Amazon CEO, replacing Bezos who is stepping down from day-to-day activity.
4. R. Martin. *M&A: The One Thing You Need to Get Right*. HBR June 2016.
5. T. Ingham. Senior research fellow in the Department of Medicine at the University of Otago in Wellington, and Executive Chair of the Muscular Dystrophy Association of New Zealand.

5

The Everyday Relationships We Fail to Recognize: Structure Is Only Half the Picture

There are two distinctive executive functions: making decisions and implementing them. Frequently, executives make great decisions, yet undercut implementation, resulting in expensive failures. Cascading plans and information fail to engage people's hearts and minds. The quality of leader-staff relationships dramatically influences performance, and results either in flying in formation or fragmentation. Management by walking around transforms from a patriarchal approach to get to know staff into leaders discovering human gems.

> The board of an SME was confident in their recent CEO appointment. He was personable, brought international experience, and had a track record of successes. The company was ripe for rapid expansion. The board was delighted with signs of early progress and his personable approach had landed well with stakeholders and suppliers. Then rumors began circulating that the head office staff were unhappy. On investigation it was discovered that staff were complaining to board members about the new CEO's manner. They were also discussing the changes underway with the former CEO. The staff were closer to board members than the CEO was. The company was fast losing traction. The informal networks of relationships had not been reset. The staff and board were functioning as if the former arrangements still existed, leaving the CEO isolated and frustrated.

DOI: 10.4324/9781003167334-5

Unwittingly, we have been distracted by formal structures in organizations. We've emphasized the leader's role as logical decision-maker at the expense of the impact of their relationships with the people they lead. We've been mesmerized by who reports to whom and their positions in the hierarchy. This has given us a false sense of certainty. What the organization chart has not given us is any sense of how people actually work together. We have diligently overlooked the myriad of informal networks of relationships—who talks with whom, who trusts whom, who knows what is going on, who knows what won't work, and who knows how to get things done. It's no surprise that the second executive function of implementing decisions has proven fraught. Leaders either don't know or don't have mastery of the levers they need to implement their decisions.

STRUCTURE IS ONLY HALF THE PICTURE

Informal networks of relationships are based on psychosocial criteria, such as trust, care, insight, helpfulness, or criticism. These attributes attract people. They're drawn to one another and they interact.

As social and psychological beings, people form emotional connections with like-minded people. Frequently, they find other areas of unexpected private common ground: from caring for an elderly parent to surviving an earthquake, from being born in a distant country to the death of a sibling, from having a peripatetic childhood to having a partner with a terminal illness. Uncovering shared experiences creates a depth of understanding of one another that explanations fail to convey. These peer-based informal connections disregard any structural lines of authority.

These work relationships look like friendships—as if people "like" one another. That may or may not be the case. More importantly, they like working together or they like working in the same organization. Their interpersonal connections are based on being understood and their differences accepted, and are differentiated from "like" or "friendship" by the more complex criteria listed above.

Informal relationships are characteristically based on authenticity and candor. They create a sense of belonging and being humanly connected to one another, regardless of the organizational structure.

Conversely, there are people who avoid others. This is a natural psychosocial phenomenon. Everyone makes interpersonal choices to accept or reject others based on conscious or unconscious specified criteria. It is normal for everyone to make both choices. Problems occur when people who "reject" one another like opposing magnetic force fields have to work together because of their functions in the organization structure.

Consider the formal organization structure as the human skeleton. The positive, negative, and neutral (potential) relationships connections are the veins and arteries which let the life blood of the organization flow. These interpersonal connections are based on people choosing whether or not they work with others. Based on the tele connections described in Chapter 2, these informal networks of peers disregard structural lines and can either help or hinder work being done. Unlike the body's system of veins and arteries, the informal organization structure is invisible.

NO SURPRISES

Smart leaders systematically develop their own informal network of trusted advisors and colleagues—their professional social atom [1]. They rely on these people to let them know any risks and alerts that might impact their work. This personal-professional network of relationships is in addition to the intelligence from their own team, boss, and peers. Leaders' new area of work is to encourage their staff to refresh and generate their own networks of relationships within the organization, so they, too, have mutually trusted relationships.

Opposite to what you might expect, "no surprises" relies on vitality within the informal networks of relationships, like the bush telegraph in the Australian outback or the grapevine as in Marvin Gaye's superb song from 1968, or the French underground in response to Germany's occupation. Informal leaders hear trends, impressions, insights and stay alert to what's coming their way. They use this to direct what they want to happen. Conversely, when formal leaders are isolated from the informal networks of interactions, they're taken aback by what appears to suddenly land on their plate. They sense peers and bosses have gone behind their backs. The examples of Ghosen and the former ANZ CEO cited in Chapter

4 are prime examples of leaders' blindness and deafness to the informal conversations and responses to their actions or lack of the same.

ALIGNING WITH THE STARS

Highly chosen for their skills and intelligence (sociotelic criteria), or highly chosen for personal attributes like insight, perceptions, trust (psychotelic criteria), informal leaders are called *sociometric stars* [2]. They know how things are done, or have access to expertise and information helpful to others. Smart leaders know who the stars are within informal networks. The stars themselves are informal leaders with a cadre of supporters who know what they think and feel about what is happening in the organization and what they want to happen. These informal leaders greatly influence organizational outcomes. Social media influencers are an obvious public source of stars on a grand scale. There are singers, actors, athletes, fashionistas, and followers of dark arts who have millions of followers. In organizations, the stars are less visible.

Smart leaders know how to make links between the informal networks and the formal structural groups. They learn to whom they should listen, whose opinion matters, who are the internal influencers, and on what basis—or they're closely connected to someone who does know. They know that the links between themselves and the informal networks are both delicate and essential for their decisions to be implemented.

NOTHING ABOUT US WITHOUT US [3]

Kara (she, her) was long-time client who is a seasoned transformational Vice President in a federal government agency. She related this story which grew from implementing the learning from our work together.

As Kara was about to begin a significant transformation project, she decided to personally meet with everyone who was likely to be impacted. She came across Bella[4] (she, her), who had been with the agency for about a year. They had met the previous year at a "welcome to staff" morning tea. Bella had said she was about to go to New York and South Africa for LGBTI+ conferences as New Zealand's representative. Kara was both supportive and encouraging. Bella warmed to Kara. This was a marked difference from an earlier employer who had requested Bella not to continue with her community activist work.

As they talked later in the kitchen, Bella let Kara know she was transgender. Kara responded and let Bella know she had a baseline understanding of some of what it means to be transgender with a former family member. As well as the transformation project, Kara was sponsor for a Rainbow network within her agency, one the agency had struggled to get going. She wanted to find out how well her agency included people who were minorities, how this network might be formed, and how it might work. She decided to discuss possibilities with Bella. Kara included a gay colleague Zac, and a member of the diversity and inclusion team. Each person shared their stories and experiences of being in public value agencies. They concluded the organization was not ready to embrace diversity. Kara, Zac, and Bella aligned in rejecting a token response and decided to begin with "education first."

Kara included Bella as an advisor in the Diversity and Inclusion group in the Organization Development team. There were many informal/underground conversations of what would work and how.

Bella posted a brief article on pronouns on the agency intranet and was astonished and delighted by the response. Several young people found the strength to identify and "came out" to her. The CEO included her pronouns in emails and posted this in her weekly update. The senior leadership team wore pink t-shirts to take a stand against homophobic bullying (Pink Shirt Day), as part of freeing the organization workplace from unwelcome or inappropriate behavior.

Keen to put the agency's diversity policy into practice, Kara asked Bella to speak to the leadership team. Instead, Bella proposed that she and Kara identify a number of young people who were in the LBGTQ+ community and arrange for the senior leadership team to meet with them where they may share their stories of growing up and being in organizations, hear and learn from the history of the rainbow community, and discuss the reason for an agency network to exist.

Through this process Kara discovered that Bella was a member of the National Commission for UNESCO, had spoken at both New Zealand's parliament and government house. Bella also provides leadership and strategy within a community group of 25 staff, including the medical arm through COVID-19, and she chairs a board of eight. She simultaneously leads, educates leaders, and influences greater inclusion within her employer's agency. She has learned to tell her story to create alignment through her vulnerability.

This is the bizarre challenge for Bella and many of the people gems who are "informal" leaders leading, influencing, and helping implement decisions generated by the organization's formal structures. In an interview Bella shares the following:

> What I do is kick the door down, step back, and encourage others to do their thing. It is challenging for anyone to be the "first person"—to start the conversation. I have a history. I have strong support around me and I've been raised in a way to be proud of myself and the decisions I make. That helps.
>
> [4]

SYSTEM FAILURE IN PLAIN SIGHT

Just like choosing players for a schoolyard sports team, the best team members in an organization are chosen for top project and agile teams. They come up with innovations for new products, systems, business growth, and savings. Why do so many innovative projects and agile teams fail? The answer is it's not the team that fails. It's their decisions and innovations that fail to be accepted structurally and implemented. They fail because the people who create and lead these teams were either never connected to the formal decision structure in the first place or failed to keep the formal decision-makers in the loop on their progress. The boundaries of decision-making were never agreed upon. The manager accountable for the performance of those working on the project doesn't see the work being done or the results don't matter to them.

Any leader who wants to influence how groups work needs to understand these inner group structures and how to work effectively. They need to know how to investigate when things go awry, how to refresh interpersonal relationships, and how to generate new relationship networks relevant to their organization's operating environment. They need to know where to look to know who else to involve from inside the organization and when to bring in outside expertise. If leaders don't do this, they are likely to repeat restrictive choices from the past.

AT THE HEART OF THE MATTER

J. L. Moreno, doctor, psychiatrist, writer, and social investigator, developed *sociometry*—the science of relationships within the field of psychodrama. This science and allied methods enable leaders to explore and "attack the problem not from the outer structure of the group, the group surface, but from the inner structure" [5].

My observations of the organizations with which I work are through the sociometrist lens. Be it with CEOs and their senior executive teams, groups of managers and staff, high-profile project teams, or collections of leaders from a wide range of sectors, the inner structure of relationships within the group at any particular time is central to the group's success. This includes who is close to whom, who is distant from whom, and on what basis. Yet this inner group structure generally remains invisible and unspoken—and rightly so. These are private and personal relationships. Two conditions make them the leader's business:

- Things go wrong
- Psychological safety needs to be built or refreshed, enabling everyone to make their best contribution

Throughout my work, I've seen poor behavior, efforts needlessly duplicated, decision-making slowed or stuck, restructurings which failed to deliver results, and leaders who refused to meet with their teams. I've learned the main cause of these failures includes either the absence of relationships or breakdowns in relationships among people.

In new groups or with new group members, the main function of the leader is to ensure new networks of connections are facilitated.

Sociometric investigations help group members be aware of the powerful forces that affect them in their relationships with one another. They begin to see the impact of conversations inside the meeting, the informal conversations outside the meeting, and who talks with whom in both settings.

By making visible and verbalizing what is happening in particular relationships, group members realize that they're not alone, but part of a shared dynamic. Armed with this information, group members feel more united within themselves. They're more likely to initiate new behaviors and create new patterns of relationships for themselves. Interpersonal information, in the form of awareness of similarities and differences—which Moreno called companion/measure—changes the receiver. People know where they stand with one another. Their worst fears may have been confirmed: they know the truth. Yet this also creates relief and a chance for a fresh approach.

I am increasingly invited into organizations to help people develop more satisfying and productive working relationships as they reshape strategy, turn around culture, or enhance exceptional performance. My observations and analyses of these situations are that it's the informal network of relationships—the "tele" relationships, who agrees with whom, and who doesn't go along with whom—which influences and controls the actions of the group.

These relationships can be enhanced, resulting in expanding executive satisfaction and productivity. It never ceases to amaze me that groups of people may have worked together for years on significant matters, yet they really know little or nothing about one another. If we are to dramatically influence business results, this has to change. Every leader needs to know how to produce networks of quality interpersonal relationships that are beneficial to implementing business decisions. They need to know how to respond to negative relationships which affect staff morale and business results.

AMBIVALENCE IN ACTION

Ambivalence occurs when there are simultaneously positive and negative tele relationships. A typical example is family violence where there are positive love relationships, yet one or more players hurt others.

In many organizations, leaders are faced with a peer or direct report who is technically brilliant, but has poor relationships with peers or alienates their staff. Typically, these specialists see themselves as victims. They blame others for their poor results. Nothing is their fault and they take no responsibility or accountability. These people tend to be overly sensitive to any suggestions for improvements, which they take as personal criticisms. Staff and peers around them withdraw. This leads to negative feelings that are manifested in excessive niceness or politeness, and results in limited compliance. The staff keep their heads down, offering few solutions to problems. They tread on eggshells so as not to offend their boss, yet they still want to be effective in their own work.

The offending executive may be creative and technically expert. Typically, they work well with their boss and they may have exceptional external stakeholder relationships. They know what works and what doesn't. Leaders hesitate to confront the offender for fear of the imagined reaction. They tend to value the offender's technical expertise at the expense of staff concerns. Essentially leaders abandon their leadership function (Figure 5.1).

Two factors align in assessing the efficacy of ambivalent relationships:

- **Empirical evidence**: We can measure the specific downsides of poor interpersonal and group relationships. E.g., in negative boss-to-staff relationships, observers note deadlines are missed, mistakes made, and there's a high percentage of rework. Staff rarely offer innovative solutions to everyday problems.
- **Observed behaviors:** These include public disagreements with peers, loudly criticizing staff in public forums, or ignoring staff when they ask questions. Staff members rarely contribute to meetings. Instead, they use their manager's time to complain about the "bully," rather than driving changes in the business. Management time is taken up with relationship repair and listening to how people feel, rather than attending to strategy or hearing how staff approach business improvements. Does this sound familiar?

Leaders don't want to rock the boat. Yet the boat is rocking anyway. Staff members withdraw their talents. Delivery is less than optimal. Most bosses fail to act until a formal complaint is activated. Immediately, staff members see leaders remaining closer to the offending executive rather than to them as team members. Executives fail to act in the best interests of staff members. These are accurate assessments: logic goes out the window.

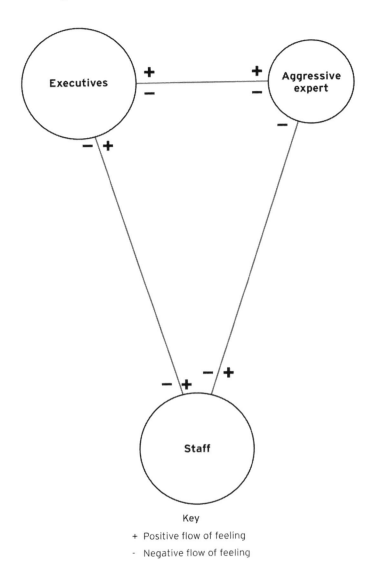

Key
+ Positive flow of feeling
- Negative flow of feeling

FIGURE 5.1
Ambivalence in structural work relationships

Individuals feel betrayed and withdraw further. They see and feel the dissonance between what the formal structure indicates—that their bosses "care" for them—yet they see bosses don't act or censure unacceptable behavior. The fear of making formal complaints results in being perceived as a trouble maker or in dismissal—and both of these frequently occur.

When bosses fail to sanction the *aggressive expert*, staff experience the dissonance between the espoused values of the organizations and the values in action. They see their bosses as weak; and they lose respect for them.

There are three principles which underpin working within informal structures:

- **Choice:** When people choose with whom they work, rather than what is dictated by the organizational structure, their capacities flourish.
- **Interventions:** Exploring existing networks or producing new ones is for the sole purpose of assisting the group's purpose and their ability to achieve the results they want.
- **Criteria:** People make choices to interact based on criteria which assist them to get their work done.

GANG BEHAVIOR VERSUS COMPANIONSHIP

Entrenched subgroups and negative interpersonal relationships within organizations disturb the work of the bigger group. Productivity grinds to a halt. A recent example was the police union within the Minneapolis Police Department at the time of the 2020 killing of George Floyd. The initial defense of the officer who caused Floyd's death was at the expense of the very people the police were there to protect. Another example is a leadership team where the CEO refused to meet with his executives because they relentlessly criticized one another. The executives refused to work together. For more than five months, the vice presidents' negative feelings about each other superseded the vision and purpose of the organization.

The new work for any group in trouble is to refresh subgroups and relationships. If this is not attended to promptly, the group disintegrates, because of the increasing isolation of one or more group members. They become focused on interpersonal relationship difficulties. Work centers around personalities who appear to have extraordinary influence over others. When coupled with managerial line relationships, schisms among leaders and staff deepen.

Within any formal structure, people are frequently drawn together on common ground through their values. Traditionally, the criteria to which people tend to gravitate are longevity in the organization, or criticism or judgment of others. They behave in ways that exclude others. When group relationships deteriorate to this point, two things happen. First, industrial or legal action dominates. Second, group members leave the group, through illness or new employment. The main task of leaders working in organizations is to bring about a greater number of positive relationships among people, enabling the relationships to be strengthened, and to help the group set new formats to ensure these new bonds are maintained.

THE BEST BUSINESS RELATIONSHIPS ARE EMOTIONAL

Contrary to business lore, emotion plays a central part in work relationships. *Trust* is a feeling of confidence and security that a partner (such as a colleague or boss) actually cares [6].

Logic may be highly valued in organizations, but there are other essential factors as well. Until the #Metoo movement, it was accepted that boards and bosses cared more for one another—and for the bottom line—than they did for their staff. This is the dynamic that gave rise to the early unions in order to protect the rights of workers because the bosses were not going to do so. Morally and ethically bereft decisions were the norm.

No more. In our current environment, caring for staff and customers has jumped the queue and now leads out from the bottom line. In 2021, the blunt and outspoken chairman of KPMG UK remarked that staff should stop acting as COVID-19 victims and simply "Get on with it" [7]. He paid the price.

The former Prime Minister of Japan and Head of the IOC noted that meetings drag on "because women talk too much and over participate" [8]. He rapidly learned that his antiquated insights and observations no longer stood scrutiny in international environments.

Neither leader alluded to or emphasized care of their staff or, in the case of the IOC, committee companions. Both lost the trust of their stakeholder constituents. Both resigned, losing significant appointments as a result. Aided by social media, the informal networks of opinion influencers are frequently stronger than any senior leader's appointed position.

PUSH THE RESET BUTTON IN INFORMAL RELATIONSHIPS

The main source of failure with new appointments, decision implementation, and restructures is leaders' failure to refresh the informal networks of relationships. They don't push the reset button. Whether within their own leadership team, within their business group, or organization-wide, leaders can stimulate new or refresh existing networks of relationships.

The simple direction, *"I want you to talk to and listen to one another about how to make this work,"* sets in motion informal relationships that stimulate alignment.

THE GLARING GAP IN BUSINESS CONTINUITY PLANNING

During the COVID-19 pandemic, the rapid adoption of remote working and physical distancing revealed glaring gaps in everyday social interactions. Leaders needed to be sociologists now more than any other time. Depleted everyday social interactions had the effect of reducing individual productivity and creativity. Many lost the ability to read their daily context and to talk with others who knew what was happening. There was a breakdown in the network of informal relationships.

Shortly after Rutherford split the atom, J. L. Moreno identified the *social atom*—the smallest number of people every person needs in order to retain their vitality, resilience, and capacity to learn. Everyone on the planet has several social atoms:

- Their *original social atom*, made up of carers, siblings, and relatives
- Their *community social atom*, made up of neighbors, friends from school, sport, and social activities
- Their *professional social atom*, made up of trusted confidants, colleagues, and bosses

The relationships among the members of each person's social atom are made up of multiple flows from attractions and rejections. These shape each person's behavior and counter-behavior and culminates in the person's cultural atom [5]. Unsurprisingly, multiple social and cultural atoms merge and collide within organizations, creating both organizational behaviors that assist work being done and behaviors which don't. The leader as sociologist needs continual courage and tenacity to have conversations to ensure everyone's behavior aligns with organizational values and the results being sought. Leaders whose mindset is *any moment is a chance to repair* feel less pressure and dismiss the notion that there's only one right time to act.

INFORMAL NETWORKS CUT ACROSS STRUCTURAL LINES

Several decades ago, it was common to see groups of smokers from an organization standing in building basements. Similarly, commuting employees frequently discussed their work experiences. Others met around the water cooler, the building kitchen, or café. Each provided an opportunity to both find out what was going on in the organization and have a chance to influence one another across hierarchical and organization lines. Chances of easy happenstance connections are fast disappearing with the shift to online interactions.

During lockdowns, there was a dramatic narrowing of relationship networks in workplaces and society. Being physically confined (either alone or in small groups at home) made many people experience their social atom being "depleted." They didn't have enough people—or perhaps the right people—around them to maintain their resilience and vitality. They are unable to make sense or learn from the setting in which they found themselves. Negative feelings toward the self and others result in cynicism, loneliness, depression, and potentially suicidal thoughts.

Employers need to rapidly find ways to help employees reconnect informally with those who are important to them. Formal structures are only part of the picture. It's the myriad of informal networks of relationships of people who *want* to work together—not because they *have* to—that is so important.

Here are 11 ways to help your people stay in the loop while working remotely:

- Run daily virtual "stand-ups" with everyone participating. Kick off with the top priorities for the day, and discuss alerts and risks.

- During high-pressure times, have a resilience readout each day using zoom polls, or personally using 'fist of five', with fingers indicating a 1–5 scale: "1" finger being *feeling low* and "5" fingers being *going well*. Leaders and peers follow up with anyone 3 and below.
- Show people how to use personal interaction tools, such as channels in Teams or Chat in Zoom, to send personal messages or questions to others in the company.
- End the day with ten minutes asking: What was satisfying? What was frustrating?
- Encourage your staff to initiate and build a personal support network using free apps. Have them choose two people with whom they wouldn't usually work, recommend a daily check-in for the upcoming weeks, and then review progress and learning.
- Set up online innovative communities of interest. Suggest three or four topics, then brainstorm with a cross section of staff. Select the best ideas and form groups, and then hold a large group debrief within four weeks.
- Encourage pictures of family and pets on your internal network.
- Conclude online town halls with random breakout rooms and lounges, in order to expand opportunities for team members to connect with others across the organization.
- Have online Friday "drinks" with a personable host.
- Set up social Facebook groups for competitions, prayers, singing.
- Offer language/learning lessons online.

Just as in-person work, it's your role to keep people connected, communicating, and caring for one another, and for the business, while they work remotely. Your team's vitality and resilience during times of reduced personal social atoms benefit both your people and the business.

THE WORLD ONCE SEEMED FLAT: WHY DO WE ACT IF IT STILL IS?

We are naive to think emotion isn't central to leaders' decision-making. Thinking, feelings, and behavior are inextricably entwined. Whitaker and Lieberman noted that behind every vision and decision toward something better, there's an opposing fear pulling in the opposite direction [1]. How well leadership teams address those fears in either the decision process or in subsequent communications dramatically influences the efficacy of the decision. If the fears of the leaders themselves (such as reputation, risk, and loss of control), their staff (job security and satisfaction), and stakeholders (having needs be met) aren't addressed, two likely outcomes result:

- Decisions are merely satisfactory, rather than exemplary
- Decision implementation causes emotional stress for one or more significant groups

Mergers and acquisitions expert Constance Dierickx developed six questions that you can ask to help sort out the effect of emotion on your decisions:

1. Am I "dead set" on a course of action? If yes, why?
2. Is there something or someone I can avoid facing if I make a particular decision? If yes, how much does that matter?
3. Have I received advice that makes me overcautious? From whom? How credible is their advice?
4. Am I being "egged on" by others? Nagged? Pushed? Why?
5. Do I hesitate because I fear using my own judgment (which has proven reliable)?
6. Looking back on the major decisions I have made, what do the good ones have in common? What do my mistakes have in common? Who can corroborate my analysis? [9]

Too often, leaders champion objectivity, facts, and information over insight, intuition, and sensing how decisions will land with their people in addition to how they'll impact the bottom line. Alternatively, they are so caught up in the emotion of a situation that their tunnel vision blinds them from exploring wider implications. By taking a step back and listening to their informal advisors as they make decisions, leaders enhance psychological safety in their organizations.

I'm not advocating decision by consensus. Not at all. Leaders are decision-makers. What I am advocating is that leaders not isolate themselves in their decision process. In the midst of the COVID-19 pandemic, American infectious disease specialist Dr. Anthony Fauci said, "I'm happy to be the skunk on the US Coronavirus Task Force." In October 2020, his view was different from those of his colleagues on that task force. Yet Fauci himself was not isolated. He was embedded in a broad network of relationships with pandemic and frontline specialists. He wasn't afraid to tell the President and Vice President of the United States what they might not want to hear:

> If you really want to know what's going on, you have got to talk to the people in the trenches. So when people were saying, "Testing is fine, everybody who wants to test can have a test," I'd get on the phone at night and talk to the individual people who are either the assistant health commissioner, the health commissioner, or somebody who's running an intensive care unit from New York [City], Chicago, New Orleans, Seattle, and Los Angeles. I'd do that regularly, and what they were seeing in the trenches was not always what was happening in the discussions. So I bring this perspective to the task force and I say, "I'm sorry, I'm not trying to undermine the president. But there is something that's called reality". [10]

What's important to note here is that the interactions Dr. Fauci describes are part of his everyday conversations within his informal network of trusted advisors.

If leaders were to ask one question of their trusted advisors as they make decisions, it should be, "With whom else do you think I should talk?"

Context change can isolate leaders. They fail to refresh who they consult with or listen to when they're in new territory. Once they're isolated and out of the loop, leaders rapidly go from knowing what's happening to seeing decisions made without their input.

JUST WHAT IS GOING ON HERE?

Over the years, I have investigated the relationship dynamics with hundreds of leadership teams. I've used similar questions each time. I can draw consistent themes from participants' responses. If more than half the group alludes to a particular matter, I assume the group is ready to discuss working with it. (Table 5.1)

TABLE 5.1

A Group Investigation Based on Six Principles

Principle	Question
Establish the team's working foundation or absence of same	What works really well in the team now?
Establish the team agenda and development priorities	What doesn't work so well that you want to address as a team?
Gain insight into new directions	How satisfied are you that the team has the right agenda? 0 —————————————— 10 Not at all very What would make your rating closer to 10?
Evaluate how effectively the expertise of each individual is utilized	How satisfied are you with your participation in team meetings and interactions? 0 —————————————— 10 Not at all very What might you contribute that would take your rating closer to 10?
Determine the current inner group structure on key criteria	To whom are you close on this team? With whom do you: • Work most? • Solve problems? • Choose as a sounding board?
Align team with the intervention's purpose and outcome being sought	If this team development was really satisfying to you, what two to three outcomes would you expect to see?

Occasionally, only one person may mention a hot item. I decide whether to alert the group leader to what's brewing to test if it's known, or to treat this as a wildcard—knowing the time isn't ripe. I have discovered it is not only business units which operate in silos. Some leaders do too. They operate as if they are self-sufficient islands. They fail to connect with the very people who hold the keys to their success

CONCLUSION

Inextricably linked, these two structures, the formal decision structure and the invisible informal can either crash into each other and disrupt action or coexist and enhance action. Leaders, it is your role to know how to tap into informal networks to benefit your employees work satisfaction, and their results.

Chapter 6 champions the power of purpose—why we do what we do.

WORKS CITED

1. D. Jones, *Leadership Material: How Personal Experience Shapes Executive Presence*, Boston London: Nicholas Brealey, 2017.
2. A. E. Hale, *Conducting Clinical Sociometric Explorations*, Roanoke Virginia: Royal Publishing Company, 1981, p. 51.
3. *Nothing about us without us*, 1990.
4. B. Simpson, Interviewee, [Interview]. March 2021.
5. J. Moreno, *Who shall survive?*, Roanoke, Virginia: Royal Publishing Company, 1993.
6. P. Thagard, "What is trust?," *Psychology Today*, 1981.
7. "KPMG's Bill Michael resigns after telling staff to 'top moaning'.," *The Guardian*, 11 February 2021.
8. "Mori's resignation highlights changing gender norms," *The Japan Times*, 26 February 2021.
9. C. Dierickx, "Your decisions are emotional," *The Board Mindset*, November 2020.
10. J. Cohen, "Why Antony Fauci is happy being the 'skunk' on the corporate task force," *Science Magazine*, October 2020.

6

The Power of Purpose

The opposite of purpose is aimlessness. Organizational contexts, structures, and operating environments continually shift and change, yet many leaders and leadership teams fail to refresh their purpose. It is at their peril that they avoid this and risk becoming outdated and irrelevant. In this chapter, we'll discuss the direct relationship between purpose and results in order to help leaders gain the trust and commitment of those they influence.

I was invited to work with a senior leadership team rife with interpersonal frustrations. They struggled to move from transactional interactions focused on their business groups. They were about to undertake a company-wide transformation with dramatically expanded services. I interviewed each team member and asked them what the purpose of the leadership team was. I was not surprised to receive five different responses. Only the CEO reflected the stated purpose of the team. I also discovered that while the leadership team had discussions, they made no business-wide decisions. Not only was the leadership purpose unclear, few related to it.

Contrast this with the *Washington Post.* In 2014, Jeff Bezos bought the *Washington Post.* He bought it because its purpose was clear as were the talents of the staff. The business was losing money "not through any fault of the people working there or the leadership team. The problem was a secular one, not cyclical.[1]" The transition Bezos saw he could help with was moving from a national newspaper to a global one, from an outdated print-based offering to free global distribution, from requiring super

DOI: 10.4324/9781003167334-6

expensive heavy capital investments to free distribution via the internet. Bezos switched the business model from making a lot of money from a small number of readers to making a little bit of money from a very large number of readers. He had the confidence to do that because the purpose of the *Washington Post* was clear, valid, and unchanged.

Many leadership teams with whom I have worked have boring or irrelevant purposes. Some have not refreshed their purpose for years, even though both team members and organization contexts have changed dramatically. The downside of ignoring "use-by dates" for team or meeting purposes means outdated practices continue. No one knows where these practices originated. More importantly, no one cares about something they know is irrelevant.

> I recently observed a senior leadership team who discovered there was no executive owner for the papers presented at their meetings. Staff would initiate papers and present them to the leadership team for decisions, yet not a single executive knew what problem each paper was resolving until they heard this at their meeting. Each leader thought *someone else* had ownership.

Why is this important? A boring team purpose generates boring interaction processes. The most boring team purpose I hear is, "We lead the *ABC* group."

Compare this with a high-functioning team which responded to feedback for being critical and judgmental: "We are great to work for and with."

Stimulated by a change in government and in team membership, the *ABC* group inspired themselves and those around them with their refreshed purpose. When team purpose enlivens executives, their staff and stakeholders notice the quality and vitality of interactions shift dramatically, as do the results the team produces.

Another leadership team fraught with interpersonal conflicts had not met for several months. This team had two charters, a set of group rules, and a values document. None of these assisted team members during this difficult period. The CEO called me in frustration because his executives couldn't bear to be in the room with one another. He'd made significant changes to the team's composition and with careful preparation, team members were ready to meet again. Their turbulent history was not lost on these executives. My work was to help reestablish their relationships, define meeting protocols, embed a culture of respect, and get consensus on their agenda. Within hours they had come up with this statement:

We inspire trust and confidence across the organization and externally. We:

- *Lead the strategic direction*
- *Monitor our results against our strategy*
- *Identify roadblocks and manage risk*
- *Embed the organizational culture*
- *Clearly communicate expectations to our staff*

Inspired purpose increases vitality and crystalizes intention in leadership teams.

FOCUS PREPARATION ON OUTCOMES, NOT CONTENT

Outcomes are close allies with purpose. Many leaders fall into the trap of focusing on the content of their agenda item but ignoring purpose and the desired outcomes. Naturally, this causes listeners to delve into both the detail of the content and the process of delivery. Recipients aren't able to retain a high level of details and facts given to them by executives who can easily be dismissed as boring and irrelevant. They fail to generate any sense of urgency, engagement, or result. These leaders fall into the knowledge and expertise trap. Their *modus operandi* is to describe, explain, and rely on the volume of information. Those around them are forced to try to remember unnecessary details and their vitality promptly withers away into boredom. The leaders forget to relate the work at hand to the outcomes they want to achieve to improve their organization's condition.

Rod Deane was Chair of Fletcher Challenge, at the time one of New Zealand's largest construction companies. He refused to read 4 inches of meticulously prepared board papers delivered the night before the board was deciding how to restructure the company.

His comment: "That's disrespectful! [2]" The executives preparing the board papers had neither taken into account the purpose of the papers nor thought about how to prepare for Deane and his fellow board members to be on top of any material. They hadn't helped the board be ready for their significant conversation and decisions.

Few people want to be held for ransom the night before a meeting by hundreds of pages of complex material which doesn't help them make decisions.

Yet volumes of papers habitually delivered at short notice remain the *modus operandi* of many business and government organizations. These signify two great failures for executives: either to purposefully commission papers or to wholeheartedly stand in the shoes of those for whom they prepare papers and perceive what they need to make wise decisions.

Successful leaders approach this quite differently. The most successful leaders I've ever seen do the following:

- They focus ruthlessly on the outcome they want for the organization and go backward from there
- They focus on futures and know the precise action they want their audience to take
- They arbitrarily choose three key priorities as messages
- They define results and don't worry about inputs
- They craft the question that mines their audience's experience and expertise

Make no mistake, this approach to preparation is hard work. But with practice, the investment of only a few minutes prior to any interaction results in high-quality conversations and decisions (refer to Figure 4.1).

This preparation is critical for any leader who wants to draw people together to create change and alignment in their organization. It results directly in bosses, staff, and peers drawing closer to the executive. It increases trust and it helps with implementing decisions, since executives are not weighed down by endless descriptions and explanations. They focus on implementing knowing their purpose, and the outcomes they want.

Within 12 hours of the March 2019 mosque attacks in New Zealand, the leadership team of Victim Support New Zealand—headed by CEO Kevin Tso—hand-picked a team of counselors from around the country and flew them to Christchurch. Each victim and their family were personally assigned a counselor who worked alongside this family for several months. Some continue to do so to this day.

At the same time, Kevin's General Manager Finance and Communication set up a Give-a-little page for public donations, expecting to attract perhaps close to $3 million dollars. The trauma and ongoing difficulties of everyone affected were not underestimated. The swift action of Tso and his organization drew over $14 million dollars in donations—dramatically increased trust and confidence in his organization, and greatly assisted in providing pragmatic and psychological care to over 1200 devastated individuals and their community.

> Our vision is to care for people and help them navigate officialdom that touches on the most personal and private aspects of their lives. Our service is as caring conduits to access services which empower victims on their journey to safety, healing and participation.
> —**Kevin Tso**

ARE YOU MORE LIKELY TO INVITE AND INSPIRE OR TO CONSULT AND MANIPULATE?

You might be thinking that as leader you know best. Occasionally, that will be true. You might be thinking, too, that involving people is the best way to proceed. That may also be true. But *how* you involve people that would lead to either alignment or alienation.

This is why your mindset must involve people in ways that are contrary to what might be expected. It's about involving them on *their* terms. Contrary to popular belief, having a consultation is *not* involving people: it's asking people to respond to your ideas and to what you think should occur. The door is already closed, and most people are aware of that.

Those being consulted will work hard to come up with reasons, options, and creative solutions to address the problems presented. None of these are likely to influence leaders, whose mindset they know best. They're playing the game of, "We know what is needed here, not you."

Cynicism and disillusion abound with those who receive these. How many burning platforms have been left in a pile of cinders, with the leader's vision going up in smoke? People know they have been manipulated and they act accordingly.

SO, WHAT *DOES* WORK?

Successful leaders have a different mindset. They know that *leading is a relationship business.* They accept that there are three entities in the relationship: themselves, the people they lead, *and* the relationship! Their purpose and mindset include and respect both people and the relationship.

Early in 2020, the New Zealand government declared a COVID-19 state of emergency. Other than essential workers (medical and food supply chain, supermarkets, enforcement agencies), all New Zealanders had to remain physically distant. Each person stayed inside their home with a few family members for four weeks. Public officials speaking on national television were exemplary with clear visions, directions, and expectations, and they gave personable responses to journalists' questions.

Sadly, though, one official called those failing to comply, "stupid people." No one will cooperate if they believe they're going to be insulted. This leader forgot that leadership is a relationship business. He acted as if, as an enforcer, he was in the insult business. Government enforcers had said they would first encourage compliance, and then issue fines. If that didn't work, they would arrest those who fail to comply. Leaders who want others to collaborate must stick to their own rules of the game. They must hold to their purpose. They should ensure that how they communicate shows their relationship with their stakeholders is valued, even when the messages are tough to deliver.

THE INVITE AND INSPIRE MINDSET

The invite and inspire mindset elicits something fresh from those who adopt it. What is this mindset and vocabulary?

Imagine this. In the face of the COVID-19 national emergency, many companies' first response was to close businesses. The CEOs saw that their business was not considered an essential service and they wanted to take advantage of any government employee subsidies. What were their options?

- Close the business, place employees on government grants.
- Close the business. Keep in regular contact with all employees and check on how they're doing. Ask them about challenges and high points.
- Keep the business open going forward. Ask employees: What's the biggest challenge you're facing and what innovations do you believe the company should adopt?

This third option was a consultation that respects and values employee input. For instance, innovations in response to COVID-19 in Aoteroa New Zealand included:

- Government payments were made within hours after requests for employee grants.
- A platform for B2B workforce exchange among organizations was developed, which allowed them to keep their existing work agreements.
- Air New Zealand created a "Staying in Touch" register where opportunities to return to the company were posted.

The dynamics of increased engagement are right under your nose. Your mindset and your language directly influence how you invite people to participate. Leaders who do this with their teams see a bigger picture. They focus on opportunities, rather than rely on what they know.

ALIGNMENT ENCOMPASSES SIGNIFICANT DIFFERENCES

How could differences be welcome, you might ask? Many leaders I meet are afraid of conflict. As soon as any pushback is on their radar, they withdraw, dominate, make premature decisions, and take control. They take pushback—or others' perspectives and opinions—as a personal attack on their ideas. They become anxious and shut down conversations. This dynamic dramatically limits quality conversations.

As I write, many parts of the world are still in lockdown in response to the pandemic. Most people in the world now have had a shared experience of being in lockdown. They are maintaining physical distance from wider family, friends, and colleagues. But physical distance doesn't mean empathy distance. Physical distance doesn't mean emotional distance from those who are important to us. In business, physical distance doesn't mean value distance.

Let me tell you how to get close to your staff, whatever the physical circumstances.

If you ask any group of staff about their experience working from home or being isolated from key colleagues and what they've done in response, each person will have a different story. What stands out to any listener are *the connections through shared experiences* among storytellers. Relaying shared experience becomes a peer consultation. The combination of individual contributions informs leaders' decision-making on the chosen topic. Who makes the decision becomes the key issue. Is it a group decision by simple majority, by intensity of feeling, the loudest voice, or is it a decision made by the boss?

At a recent breakfast e-meeting, a group of regional businesswomen shared their experiences in rapidly shifting their businesses online. There were hoteliers, accountants, school principals, financial experts, a governance specialist, office managers, an artist, and a transport company owner. Each had vastly different experiences and challenges. Two common themes stood out: sharing a physical space under extreme circumstances and grappling with the use of new technology to maintain contact with staff and family. The shared interest and central motivator for these businesswomen were in simply hearing one another's experience. This group became aligned in their drive to find solutions. They'd accessed sources of expertise to keep both their businesses and themselves flourishing. The meeting leader's role was to simply facilitate the discussion. Subsequent action relied on the individuals to apply what they had learned in the conversation, or to initiate discussions with other group members, specifically to request needed assistance for their unique situation.

It's not the quality of facts and information that helps decision-making. It's the quality of the *questions* the executives and staff are asked that shapes the power and relevance of their contributions.

To flourish in this context, executives need to develop the capacity to:

- Distill disparate perspectives
- Find themes
- Pinpoint significant or competing differences
- Assess key people influencers
- Read and respond to the feeling level of interactions
- Take stock of roadblocks
- Identify gaps
- Crystalize implications of the decision through strategy

Currently, I am one of three people coordinating an annual conference for trainer development for an Australian/New Zealand professional association. This subgroup of trainers has met annually for almost 30 years. We meet and live-in at a venue from a Wednesday evening to a Sunday afternoon each September. This event guides and stimulates our camaraderie, organizational development, curriculum development, and best practice for the ensuing year. During the pandemic, we decided on Plan A and Plan B. In Plan A, we would meet physically; with Plan B, we'd meet electronically.

After early consultations, we noticed a major shift regarding two agenda items: organizational development, and our response to COVID-19. That was it. I noticed how easy it was to make this decision. The purpose of our team was clear.

An oyster turns a piece of grit into a pearl, but organizational silos will always remain annoying grit.

A business improvement team became isolated and increasingly irrelevant to the business.

My initial interviews revealed communication breakdowns within a leadership team. Poor staff engagement kept the focus of the leadership team on competitive infighting and interpersonal clashes. Essential internal stakeholder relationships were lost.

I initially led a rapid rebuilding of relationships among the leadership team. We established shared priorities. I coached the leader to stop being overly consultative and to shift to sharing her vision, direction, and expectations. To her credit, she did this.

We shifted the team agenda from a discussion of planning methodology—which was at the heart of many disagreements—to a focus on leaders' coaching staff, prioritizing business development decisions, and reporting results.

The lead team let staff know they wanted to:

- Increase their engagement
- Coach and develop them
- Enable greater collaboration
- Do the right thing by customers
- Enable staff feedback and decisions

The leaders wanted to restructure the group with themselves as coaches, rather than the current orientation as project leaders.

I cautioned not to proceed with a formal restructure where leaders would decide who would be on each team and I counseled against using a formal restructuring process for three reasons. First, the tedious process wouldn't produce the result they wanted. Second, HR would likely complicate the process, rather than facilitate it. Third, this time-consuming process would delay rapidly needed stakeholder relationship repairs and negatively impact business results.

I proposed instead that team members choose their leader in situ based on the leader's focus and coaching emphasis.

The initial push against this proposal was strong. I listened to the leaders' concerns. *What if people wanted to change teams after the decisions?* I proposed a simple process for people who wanted to change teams later.

The second strongest concern was, *What would HR say?* I asked them how helpful had HR been leading up to the current situation. Leaders were torn, as several had good relationships within HR, but they realized those good relationships hadn't helped resolve the problems. One leader said, *"What have we got to lose? If it doesn't work, we can go the formal way."* The decision was made: The staff would choose their leaders and their team colleagues.

With a clear purpose in mind, the leadership team agreed to five selection criteria to get the proper balance on each team:

- Have a minimum of three senior leaders on each team.
- Ensure teams are more or less equal in the number of members.
- Maintain a balance of design, improvement, and coaching expertise in each team.
- Make the best decision for your group and for yourself in selecting a coaching relationship and your team peers. *Note:* This is *not* selecting the projects on which you work.
- Have as much fun as you can—this is experimental, and we are innovating!

At an in-person meeting, of 64 people stood in a large circle with the six leaders out front. Each leader spoke in turn about five of their main qualities, three areas of expertise, and the emphasis they would take as coaches. Staff then chose for whom they wanted to work. Each person physically moved to stand around their chosen leader. I invited people to look around and try out a second group. Several did this. The new teams then sat together and introduced themselves to one another.

In two-and-a-half hours, the new teams were formed and consolidated. Three people changed teams later that week after discussion and agreement with the team leader.

Within weeks, early successes included:

- Complicated workarounds were retired, returning processes to their simpler state
- The triage function was humming
- Performance reporting was automated and completed in a few minutes, rather than weeks
- The backlog of improvement requests was reduced from 90 to 23 in just three months
- Stakeholders reported greater satisfaction

Staff members respond to leaders who have a clear purpose, criteria for making choices, a high trust mindset, and language to match. In these conditions, both leaders and staff generate, accept, and implement innovative solutions.

KEEPING YOUR EGO OUT OF THE EQUATION

Leaders who are subject matter experts are deeply challenged by this proposition. They are pulled in at least two directions. First, they believe they're sought out because of their expertise. This is a deeply satisfying experience, as it shapes their professional identity and feeds their ego. The second is that their task is to develop others. This often stymies them.

Geoff is a senior leader who was grappling with this. "My role is to be a subject matter expert," he told me.

My response:

Leading people is not giving them your precise knowledge. Leading people is teaching and coaching them to think as you do. You would coach others how to think from their stakeholders' perspective. They would stand in the shoes of each stakeholder and see through their eyes, to see what they see.

I continued:

What are the questions to which your stakeholders want responses? You would coach your leaders to think two or three steps ahead of that question. Do this, and your team will take initiatives and have greater confidence. Your own focus could shift to removing roadblocks and implementing strategy.

Leaders who teach their staff to think as they do dramatically increase their influence, are trusted more by their staff, and build greater leadership capacity within their team.

The second area where leaders' egos need to shift into the background in order to fulfill their purpose is in their communications. Diana, Princess of Wales, famously said, "There are three of us in this relationship." This aptly describes how many leaders work. There's the leader, their ego, and

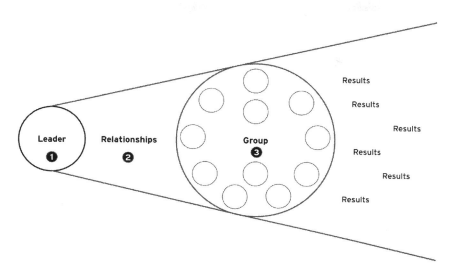

FIGURE 6.1
Three entities in leaders' relationships

the person or group with whom they're working. An essential mindset for influential leaders is to firmly place their egos in the background (Figure 6.1).

Leaders who use leadership levers will need to ensure that both their mindset and their language are tuned to the relationship between their team members and the outcomes they want. The quality of the relationship must be the third entity between any leader and their groups.

ALIGNMENT ENCOMPASSES SIGNIFICANT DIFFERENCES

The biggest mistake made by leaders and participants is assuming they have to give up their opposing points of view in order to align in direction. Successful leaders know how to help people align by accepting the differences of others. They don't expect people to give up their own identities. Instead, they uncover new territory to establish common ground, and this becomes the source for alignment.

Here are two examples.

EXAMPLE 1

During the early months of the COVID-19 pandemic, several long-standing high-performing New Zealand government leaders were invited to lead other cross-government functions. Within the ensuing months, these team members lost contact with their team colleagues. Their original team priorities were no longer relevant.

Some team members remained in the central office to lead business as usual for the group, assisted by others who stepped up as needed. Months later, when the pandemic response was normalized, their vice presidents recalled their direct reports to reestablish their teams and shape their path forward. I was brought in help refresh many of the team relationships and guide their strategies going forward.

Team members hadn't seen one another for several months, as they were either working remotely or one of the few essential workers who worked in the office. Everyone had been in a personal bubble. For most, their professional bubbles had narrowed, or were new. Some interpersonal connections had been lost.

My initial interviews revealed several trends:

- Each team member had powerful experiences that went beyond what they had previously known
- They had successfully rapidly responded in high stakes settings and delivered the complex messages which shaped the government's response to COVID-19 in a wide range of settings
- They had significant insights into failures in cohesive responses, including working with private sector entrepreneurs which had caused values clashes and duplications
- The experience of working remotely brought life to future possibilities for how the organization and the public sector might work more effectively together in the future
- There was an excitement for many leadership teams to capitalize on opportunities while addressing burning issues, including a determination not to revert to the old ways or roll out the same old things

Similar to working with traumatic organization events, I took the approach of tapping into their disparate experiences as a way for team members to reconnect. With both intact teams and my public seminars, these sessions were online. In each session, I invited executives to take six minutes each and share their experience of being in new territory, as well as what they had learned about themselves as leaders. The leaders heard one another's experiences for the first time. Their mastery of complexity inspired. The challenges resonated. Their frustrations signaled areas where changes could be made for the future. The learning varied. These sessions were nothing short of magical. The self-disclosure and authenticity of each leader radiated. Earlier strong mutual connections sprang back to life and became strengthened. Within a few hours, these executives and their leader were ready to repurpose their work teams to be more relevant and refresh their business strategies going forward.

Executives sharing their experience, insights, and reflections are a powerful source of human and business connections. These group conversations are not agenda-driven, yet they result in relationship-building among those present, which, in turn, drives business results. A simple goal of "regroup, refresh, refocus, and respond" after crises lays the foundations for teams to reconnect in ways that help make sense of their varied experiences and subsequently lift their game.

EXAMPLE 2

I was invited to help reform a leadership team after it was decimated by breaches of ethical behavior and poor managerial performance. The wider group had lost respect for its leaders. My focus was on helping form a cohesive leadership team respected by the wider group and trusted by the organization to deliver business results. There were only three managers from the original eleven, including one who was recently appointed. The group was diverse, i.e., half the group included people born in countries other than New Zealand. One half of the group were women; the remainder were men. One quiet male leader was close to retirement; two others were in their first managerial roles. I was aware that at least one manager had a fraught history with the Group Manager. Recently appointed team members were keen to work with that manager.

I invited the leaders to share a story which had influenced them as leaders. The stories were fascinating. The leaders built a depth of knowledge about each other. Yet the stories emphasized significant differences rather than creating connections and common ground.

Over lunch, I listened to their conversation. They were discussing outdoor adventures they'd had in New Zealand. I heard strong responses, such as "I would never do that," as one manager discussed his experience of sky diving. "I would never do that either! I've bungee jumped, yes. But sky diving? No."

We gathered after lunch and I set out a physical continuum at the front of the room about the criterion of risk. I knew this group's appetite for risk was going to be important, as they charted their way forward, rebuilt their reputation, and improved their relationships across the organization.

I invited people to take a position on this continuum of risk: *Those of you who love risk, stand on the right end. Those of you who are risk averse, stand on the left end.* I let group members decide whether they applied this criterion to outdoor adventure risk or risk in their personal lives. Group members were spread out along the line. We could all see there was a wide range of risk preferences. I invited group members to share why they were standing at that specific position on the line.

The stories tumbled out—from the exhilaration of flying free in outdoor pursuits to fear and anxiety from not having their feet firmly on the ground. Ben, the eldest manager, shared his story. *I can't stand physical risk. The biggest risk I ever took was with my wife. I met her when I was 18, and knew she was the one for me. I asked her to marry me within three weeks. We are celebrating our 47th anniversary later this year.* At that moment, the group burst into applause. They softened and formed mutually positive relationships with Ben and with one another. We were ready to shift our attention to the group's purpose.

The leaders knew there was a rift between themselves as the leadership team and their direct reports. Departmental meetings were described as tedious and uninspiring. Rather than being downhearted, this group of leaders was motivated and wanted both their relationships and departmental relationships to be characterized by trust, respect, and engagement. This leadership team wanted to be known for their simple, clear, succinct communications. We were ready to get work.

To lead their department in this new period, they decided their purpose was to really connect with their staff: *You feel inspired and confident to be the best you can be. We have your back and together we create the department where you love to be a member.*

This team decided to take turns leading departmental meetings. They created a policy of involving their own teams in designing meetings, with the General Manager, reestablishing his relationship with the wider group. The General Manager began the sessions with five minutes focused on updates in direction, welcoming new team members, and acknowledging the team's successes over the past month.

This leadership team's clarity and commitment to live their purpose drove their interactions. Within three months, they were hearing from staff who looked forward to their interactions in the departmental meetings.

CONCLUSION

Clear purpose radiates a leader's intention. At the macrolevel, the main lever leaders have to continually move and respond to changes to refresh their leadership team is purpose. The worst response to change is to have your leadership team operating with an outdated or bland purpose. Create unity in direction with a powerful purpose that inspires both you and your staff.

Chapter 7 applies the power of purpose at a microlevel—in meetings and interactions. We outline the principles and processes every leader should apply and ensure that both they themselves and their people love being in their meetings and are excited about the results they produce.

REFERENCES

1. Walter Isaacson. *Invent and Wander: The Collected Writings of Jeff Bezos.* Harvard Business Review Press & Public Affairs, 2021, p 218.
2. Wallace, Bruce. *Battle of the Titans: Sir Ronald Trotter, Hugh Fletcher and the rise and fall of Fletcher Challenge.* Penguin Books: New Zealand, 2001.

7

Generating Seismic Shifts with Fine Touches

Leaders who make small shifts in how they work with groups can release their team members' desire and capacity to participate and contribute to exceptional results. Expect vitality to underpin in your interactions, and refuse to be trapped by behavior patterns that have passed their use-by-date.

In Chapter 3, I wrote of the leader using the right *sockets* to work well with groups. When leaders use specific principles and processes in their interactions, they are likely to power up and achieve the results they want. In this chapter, we'll discuss six seismic shifts, their allied processes, and give examples. In Chapter 3, we saw the greatest shift for leaders is from preparing content and knowledge to focusing on accessing participants' capacities. Leaders do this through their relationship with participants, by operating as a catalyst for relationships among participants. In this chapter, we discuss how the greatest shift for leaders is from being creatures of habit to thoughtfully working with six seismic shifts focused on both the leader's relationship with participants and the relationships among participants themselves.

The great leap for authoritarian, chaotic, and habitual leaders who want to lead great meetings is to develop a behavioral mindset. Imagine, for example, you are the welcoming inclusive host, an appreciative peer, the accountable direction setter, the wise insightful talent spotter, the succinct purposeful visionary, the inviting navigator, the astute question designer, and the ruthless personable conductor.

These leadership behaviors result in participants being wholeheartedly present. Participants make a transition from their previous interactions,

DOI: 10.4324/9781003167334-7

which might be anything from hearing of a failed budget bid to leading a tricky performance conversation, being in an intense board meeting, or worrying one of their children isn't well and needs attention. Contrast this with leaders who dive into the contents of their meeting before everyone has mentally arrived. They may be there physically, but mindfully and wholeheartedly—they're all somewhere else. A transition to a new work meeting takes several minutes for most people.

Anything less than these behaviors results in either compliant participants or people who become defensive. The wide range of defensive behaviors comes to the fore. Leaders need to ensure everyone is welcomed, included, accepted, and confident their contribution will be heard. When this doesn't happen, the result is personal chaos, and participants warm up to fighting the leader, and anyone who aligns with them.

Ground rules don't work. As soon as tensions rise, the carefully agreed compliant behaviors fly out the window.

SEISMIC SHIFT 1: FROM FOLLOWING THE AGENDA TO SHAPING THE FIRST FOUR MINUTES—SIX PRINCIPLES FOR POWERFUL PURPOSEFUL MEETINGS

In practice, these six principles take the first four minutes of each of your meetings. There are two areas of concentrated preparation:

- Deciding the *outcome* you want from each meeting.
- Clarifying a simple worthwhile *process* for people to make their best contributions with each agenda item.

THE SIX PRINCIPLES FOR POWERFUL GROUP INTERACTIONS AND ENGAGEMENT

The role of the leader here is to help participants *arrive* and warmup to you as leader, to the setting, the purpose of their interactions, and their own valuable contributions. They will then make the transition to the current setting and see how their contributions will influence outcomes that are also important to them.

The six principles come through your metacommunication to your group—a communication about what is going to happen and how people can contribute, rather than just diving in haphazardly. This approach addresses each of Schein's interpersonal needs of inclusion or identity, controls influence and power, and acceptance and intimacy, outlined in Chapter 3.

1. Begin with an Inclusive Welcome

Two interwoven ideas form beginnings. The first is that the leader has the function as the *welcoming inclusive host* and the second is that *every moment is a chance for a fresh beginning.*

The best way to mark a fresh beginning is to know who's with you and to welcome each and every one of them. The most simple beginning is: *Hello everyone.* Other welcomes don't work. *Hi* is informal and warms people up to social interactions, rather than to purposeful work interactions. *Good morning* or *good afternoon* rockets everyone back to school days and you'll more than likely hear *Good morning, Miss,* or *good afternoon, Sir* in response.

Most will have come directly from other meetings or interactions. The inclusive welcome marks the beginning of a fresh interaction, and most likely a new purpose. This enables people to begin their transition to this new purpose.

2. Express Your Appreciation

Simple is best here. *Thank you for coming,* or *thank you for being here.* Staff who know they are appreciated are more motivated, more productive, and go the extra mile. Leaders can ensure everyone brings their best to group interactions and decisions by a simple expression of appreciation.

Simple, sincere appreciations appear as social niceties, yet are powerful motivators.

3. Consolidate Your Relationship with the Group as Leader with an "I" Statement

Here, leaders make an easy self-disclosure and affirm themselves in their relationship with the group:

> *I am pleased to see you all here.*
> *I am looking forward to our conversation today.*
> *I am excited we are grappling with what is in front of us.*
> *I am looking forward to taking our next step with XXX.*

This is the moment you identify as the leader and participants settle in to being listeners or contributors. Oddly enough, many leaders completely fudge this step. Rather than being accountable and using the assertion "I," they default to passive language and use "It." They overlook this opportunity for leadership. Meeting participants feel disappointed in the lack of leadership, and in not being acknowledged. The rot sets in from there.

A sincere and simple "I" statement builds participants' sense of appreciation of you as leader, engenders their confidence that you are in control, and consolidates your working relationship with them.

4. Show Your Respect for Group Members by Acknowledging Their Experience and Expertise

When you omit this step, participants feel taken for granted. They sense leaders have gone one-up, and put them one-down. They feel dominated. Their default response is to warm up to be competitive, aggressively fight, or "absent" themselves and not bother participating. They lose interest in finding common ground or developing innovative solutions. Opportunity is lost.

The beginning of every meeting is another chance for leaders to set peer interactions in place where everyone who wants to contribute can do so. Examples include:

- *Each of you brings a depth of expertise and experience which helps us tackle what is in front of us.*
- *I know each person has had ideas and experience which we need in order to create a breakthrough in this area.*

- *I am confident that the talent around this table will land us where we want to be.*

> Dominic chairs a local college board in a fast growing suburb. Their meeting is focused on strategy. They anticipate rapid growth in student numbers in their school over the next five years, with large numbers of residents choosing this attractive location. He acknowledges to his board,
>
> > "Each of you brings a breadth and depth of experience of this community and the power of education to this conversation. Your hopes for your own children and your vision for future students in our area will shape how you think about how this college can continue to ensure our students flourish."

5. Identify the Purpose of the Meeting and/or the Outcome

This is the "Tadah!" moment—the reason why people have gathered together, either online or in person. It's the chance to make everyone's commitment worthwhile. It's the moment you and the group commit to align and work together.

Chapter 6 championed the power of purpose. At a microlevel, identifying purpose and/or outcomes of every agenda item brings vitality to meetings. People shift from being automatons to accessing their spontaneity. Who would have thought! Like each of you, I have been to thousands of meetings. I can identify only a handful of leaders who began their interactions with a clear purpose or outcome.

The distinction between purpose and outcome is both slim and helpful. *Purpose* identifies an intention. *Outcomes* have a specific measurable result expressed, as if it's already a fact. I focus on agenda items and meeting outcomes using a past tense verb.

By the end of this meeting we will have:

- Established ...
- Clarified ...

- Implemented …
- Found a way forward …
- Resolved …
- Taken the next step toward …

Ensure any written agenda states the outcome being sought within each item.

6. Outline a Process for Participation

Why is it that so many meetings go awry? Levels of meaningful participation are low. Participants tend to replicate default survival behaviors from earlier experience of family mealtimes, their cultural settings, major life events, or their former early school days. They dominate by overtalking and overparticipating, or remain silent and watchful—all the time wishing they were somewhere else.

Without structure for people to participate, it's no wonder meetings don't work.

When the leader gives clear direction for processes to participate, people know how to collaborate. The leader's direction can be as simple as the following:

I'll take five minutes to discuss the major benefits to the business and how we can navigate the roadblocks. Then I'll invite each of you to make your best contribution on the impact on your area as we discuss how to best implement this.

And there you have it. This is the preparation for leaders who want to have powerful, purposeful interactions in group settings. For both online and in-person meetings, my best advice for presenters and meeting chairs is to use these six principles to lead the first four minutes of every meeting. The outcomes are that people are individually welcomed, the relationships between staff and the leader are clear. When team members know their efforts to make the meeting a priority are appreciated, they become present both personally and professionally. In knowing their contributions are being sought and how they can contribute, everyone relaxes confident they are in for a purposeful satisfying meeting (Table 7.1).

TABLE 7.1

The Six Principles of Exceptional Meetings

Principle	Example
An inclusive welcome	Hello everyone
Appreciation	Thank you for coming
Personal communication	I am pleased to see you all here, and I'm excited about the work we have ahead of us
Acknowledgments	I know each and every one of you brings considerable experience and expertise to our work together
The outcome or purpose of the meeting	The purpose of this meeting is to ... By the end of this meeting, we will have: • Established ... • Clarified ... • Implemented ... • Discovered a way forward ... • Resolved ... • Taken the next step toward ...
A process for participation	Let those there know how you want to proceed: *I'm going to share my vision with you for ten minutes, then I want to hear a response from each of you. What resonated with you? Was there anything that made your heart sink?*

SEISMIC SHIFT 2: FROM LEADERS AS MEETING MANAGERS TO LEADERS AS GUARDIANS OF GROUP DEVELOPMENT

Leaders, it's up to you to be the guardian of your group's development. Logic won't help you, but your intelligence, insights, perception, and spontaneity will. *Spontaneity* is the capacity to respond to both new and familiar formerly unworkable situations with vitality, adequacy, innovation, creativity, and flexibility. These five elements differentiate impulsiveness—a rapid response without thought—from spontaneity.

Leaders who unwittingly overlook their role as guardians of people and group development frequently discover "people problems," which in turn dominate their thinking and emotional energy. The moment people *feel* excluded, their psychological fuse is blown. They rapidly shift from resourceful beings to reactive warriors. They behave as if their lives and freedom are under threat. They revert to default behavior learned in their childhood or teenage years, in response to threatening situations. The amygdala within the brain takes over conscious thought and they respond in one of three ways:

- **Fight**—through shouting, aggression, sabotaging the meeting, or undermining the leader
- **Flight**—"leaving" through silence, illness, or physically removing themselves from the situation
- **Freeze**—become immobilized in shock, as if they are a deer in the headlights

We've all been in meetings where participants shout, verbally insult or attack one other, refuse to listen or engage, or remain watchful and silent.

What might account for this kind of aggression in organizations?

In my book *Leadership Material* [1], I wrote of the influence of childhood experiences on leaders' behavior. Under pressure, leaders tend to default to coping behaviors, which result in taking themselves toward people, moving away from people, or moving against people when the chips are down.

Group behavior is similar. Each of us is affected by our early experiences with groups, particularly our original family, school, and social activities. As leaders become more senior, the influence of hierarchical relationships under stress can bring out old responses. This surfaces when they lose out on a much-wanted appointment or during mergers, acquisitions, and restructurings where structural relationships change. This causes stress in reforming relationships with someone with whom they may not have worked previously. New team members joining groups can create competitiveness in others, as everyone jockeys for position with the boss.

Leaders who are overly authoritarian, impersonal, or chaotic in leading meetings unwittingly replicate conditions for others, which reminds them of earlier experiences where they learned to survive by coping. Most executives develop capacities to flourish in wide-ranging situations. Others don't.

Original family structure and parenting circumstances can strongly influence executive behavior. UK psychologist and psychoanalyst John Bowlby examined the impact of parenting approaches on subsequent relationship behavior. Bowlby's *attachment theory* helps describe the possible causes of aberrant executive behaviors. He brought to light the deep emotional attachment between the caregiving parent and a child. Bowlby identified at least three forms of relationship behavior:

- Children who are *nurtured and cared* for as babies form secure attachments.
- Those who were *neglected or abandoned* tend to be anxious or detached in forming relationships.
- Those who had *inconsistent care or abuse* by angry parents, tend to avoid forming relationships [2].

Cindy Hazan and Phillip Shavers' 1990s UK research into love relationships revealed 56% of adults were likely to be securely attached, 24% avoided attachment, and 20% were anxiously attached [3]. If this is reasonably accurate and could be extrapolated to both work relationships and other countries, it means leaders have much to learn in understanding their team members and shaping group behavior.

When parachuting, there always comes a time where you let go and jump free. Leading groups is similar, in that at some point you also must let go and jump. It's the only way—knowing you have the rip cord close by to pull when needed, and can control the nature of your trip down to earth and how and where you land. Adopting the mindset that *every moment is a chance for repair* immediately makes the leader's life easier. The leader knows they can choose when to pull the rip cord, make a fresh beginning, and create spontaneous interventions.

This is the moment to accept that you don't need to have all the answers. You no longer work from memory or default habits. Your job as leader is to hold the vision, decide direction, give clear expectations, and define what success looks like. When this goes to plan, those around you will do the rest.

SEISMIC SHIFT 3: FROM KNEE-JERK INTERACTIONS TO METACOMMUNICATION—OPEN THE DOOR BEFORE YOU WALK DOWN YOUR OWN RED CARPET

Too often leaders leap straight into their message without indicating their intention or conveying their relationship message to receivers. This works well in strong peer relationships. Albert Mehrabian discovered that, whether we like it or not, how we communicate conveys our feelings and attitudes toward the recipient [4]. Leaping in doesn't work in those interactions where leaders want recipients to respond, rather than just react.

Metacommunication is a communication about your communication. Here, you are laying down the carpet and inviting others to walk on it with a specific purpose in mind. Without this step, participation is likely to be knee-jerk, haphazard, and purposeless. Leaders often expect their team to read their minds and work out what the leader wants. They forget their team members are not mind readers.

In their *Harvard Business Review* article, "Stop the Meeting Madness," Perlow, Hadley, and Ein report survey results of 182 senior managers in a range of industries: 65% said meetings keep them from completing their own work; 71% said meetings are unproductive and inefficient; 64% said meetings come at the expense of deep thinking; 62% said meetings miss opportunities to bring the team closer together [5].

This sample was small, but the results are widely reflected in many organizations with whom I consult. "The hard truth is, bad meetings almost always lead to bad decisions, which is the best recipe for mediocrity."— Patrick Lencioni [6]

This does not mean leaders can't lead. What leaders should do is declare the rules for engagement: *If you raise your voice in anger, or are aggrieved, I'll interrupt you, and if you speak longer than two minutes, I will mute you.* Sanctions like this are essential for meetings to work well.

Leaders need to determine the best timing for difficult conversations. Leaders risk shaming a participant when they choose to be personally critical or when they sanction individuals in a public forum. These tough conversations are best done one-on-one soon after the offending event. Essentially, the relationship between the offender and the leader, or the offender and one or more of their colleagues, has been disrupted and broken down. A negative flow of feeling from the offender dominates. This is the area that should command the leader's attention. If it's not attended to rapidly, the leader is likely to lose hours to emotional turmoil before being able to take action. This puts delivering results at risk, as attention is diverted from the work of the group to discussing the impact of the individual's behavior.

You are responsible for your organization's culture and operating environment. Learning how to sanction individuals is firmly in your territory. You have a range of language tools, such as:

> *I want you to tone down the volume of your voice and your critical observations. You will dramatically increase your impact on our results if you do.*

Or:

> *I want you to be more successful in your relationships. Currently, you're treating your peers as if they are your slaves. They're not. I want you to be an ally—including when you disagree with them. Rather than accuse them of being stupid or that their ideas are wrong, I want you to use your insights into what will work.*

Or:

> *I want you to stop berating people. I want you to take people with you when you have a different point of view. You will have far greater influence with what you are passionate about if you let people know what is important to you rather than what you think about their ideas.*

These examples include two elements: a relationship message to the receiver that you care and your assessment and expectations as the leader (where the focus is content). Forget feedback. This is perceptive coaching using metacommunication.

SEISMIC SHIFT 4: FROM ASSUMING JOB TITLES ARE ENOUGH TO INSPIRING INTRODUCTIONS

Leaders who are approaching new groups should include an additional step, alluded to in Chapter 1. This applies to any group when any one of these conditions are present:

- The leader isn't known to participants
- Participants are new to one another
- New members join the group

Since the financial crises, rapid contextual changes have often caused unstable leadership team membership. Prior to that, it was common for leadership teams to retain the same members for decades. Mergers, acquisitions, rapid business developments or failures, and increasing uptake of small group systems, like Scrum and Agile, signal to people that they need to get to know one another rapidly. Introductions take on greater significance. Ongoing introductions are relevant, as group membership changes and new people bring additional expertise and experience.

Rather than taking years to get to know one another and work well together, introductions need to be rapidly and regularly expedited. In Chapter 1, we downgraded job function as an essential feature of introductions. Of greater significance are personal qualities, attributes, and experience relative to the task at hand.

Currently, I am working with a group of five leaders who don't know each other, as they develop a greater executive presence. Early on in the initial session, before the participants even learned each other's names, I invited them to each share a story of a moment when they first realized they were a leader. I asked, *How old were you when you realized this? Where were you geographically in the world? What was happening around you?* Up to this point, the main development theme in the group had been, *How do I more effectively influence senior leaders?*

Here's what they shared:

Leader 1 had trained in engineering and graphic design. Initially employed within geosciences, she now leads the web design team in a federal agency.

Leader 2 originally trained as a land surveyor and then led a team creating oceanic hydrographical charts to help government make better decisions on marine environments. Astutely empathetic and self-aware, this leader radiated her determination to make things happen.

Leader 3 had undergraduate degrees in history, classics, and law. Funny, perceptive, and forthright, she brought ten years of experience as a senior associate at a top UK law firm.

Leader 4 had started her career in science and pharmaceuticals, and worked in the biotech industry, including seven years in manufacturing with companies such as Pfizer and Johnson & Johnson. She had successfully led a major product development with international success and was now Quality Manager in a completely different sector.

Leader 5 had a double degree in history and criminology. She brought experience of retail banking and within the oil industry, before reforming a group that had been decimated after a senior leader had committed fraud. She rebuilt the reputation of her group, and had helped the newly appointed CEO and the organization reorient after the resulting financial and relationship devastation. She was calm in crises, learned from childhood, and is a trusted confidant and professional advisor to many senior leaders.

Learning their backgrounds allowed the group to make new interpersonal connections and better understand and assist each other. What we discovered was they had significant shared qualities and experiences:

- As senior leaders delivering exceptional results without appointed authority or mandate
- Not being managed, guided, or led, despite being in leadership roles central to their organizations' results and reputations
- Resilience, perseverance, and retaining focus under exhausting conditions

Their organizations and peers were largely unaware of these significant experiences, qualities, and the backgrounds these leaders brought to their work. Outsourced recruitment exacerbated frustration that candidate's resumes were read by recruitment agencies, not by the employing manager. Leaders can provide repeated opportunities for staff to bring forward their experience and expertise throughout their employment, not just when they join the organization.

INTRODUCTIONS THAT CREATE GROUP VITALITY AND UNITY

How do you create powerful breakthrough relationships and rapidly release talents within a group? Here are some examples:

- Board and executive members were invited to introduce themselves with the three qualities or experiences they brought to the Board's work
- Pop-up groups and project team members were asked to identify three skills and experiences they bring that will help achieve the outcome being sought

- Board members were invited to indicate why this board's function was important to them, and the legacy they wanted to leave from their work
- Task force members were invited to indicate what motivated them to contribute to the specific area
- In resolving a fraught situation, team members were invited to begin with one experience and three attributes they bring with them to resolve difficult situations.

All these introductions require self-disclosure, which rapidly increases the group's knowledge about one another, and enables group members to make interpersonal connections based on their own experience. They also deepened the level of sincerity of discussions and the level of collegial intimacy, while increasing their commitment to get to the heart of the matter.

Leaders can create their own password to Aladdin's cave and hear for themselves the gems group members bring.

THE FACELESS BUREAUCRAT'S CHOICE: TO BE INVISIBLE OR BE ACCOUNTABLE?

When leaders open meetings and presentations with the six principles, this dramatically shows their visibility and accountability. Leaders are no longer able to hide behind uncertainty and lack of commitment. Being purposeful and taking accountability for the experiences and outcomes people experience in your meetings lifts your reputation. People love being in meetings you lead. They know their contributions are sought, valued, and that they influence outcomes. This is the time for faceless bureaucrats to unmask and bring their authentic selves forward.

SEISMIC SHIFT 5: FROM RUNNING OUT OF TIME TO THREE PRINCIPLES FOR CONCLUDING MEETINGS

1. Ensure everyone leaves your meetings knowing what's been agreed upon, the unresolved significant challenges and differences, and what

the next steps are. This is achieved when the leader summarizes key outcomes. Alternatively, if you as the leader have been caught up in meeting content, ask someone else to summarize. Choose the person who looks animated. If you sense their summary is incomplete ask, *Would anyone want to add to this?* This step ensures everyone is on the same page and they are more likely to take the agreed actions.

2. Regardless of how the meeting has gone, thank everyone for their contributions. This step is essential to reiterate your appreciation.
3. Signal the next step or next meeting.
   Thanks, everyone for your participation, our next meeting is ...

RINSE AND REPEAT FOR ONLINE MEETINGS

Successful online meetings require precisely the same principles. The process for participation is emphasized. Leaders and participants gain greater value in outcomes by considering the best preparation prior to getting together. For strategy sessions, this can be accomplished with perceptive online questionnaires. Ask questions that guarantee thoughtful preparation and encourage executives to come up with innovative solutions to their organizational dilemmas. My Australian colleague Andrew Hollo, a trusted advisor to public value agencies and an online strategy expert, successfully uses *Typeform* to access group information.

Typical strategy session preparation questions that Andrew asks are as follows:

- What is the reason for your existence?
- What do you do exceptionally well? How do you know?
- What do you want that you don't have now? [7]

Online preparation replaces previous time-consuming interviews and enables a high-value focus on assessments and shaping opportunities for participation.

I invited participants to share a five-minute self-presentation video for development programs. For group case study consultations, I suggested participants submit a diagram showing the current relationship dynamics they wanted to address and encouraged them to give their diagram a compelling title.

By the time we meet, significant insights have been gained and action is catalyzed. Our work is already underway.

YOUR ONLINE TOOLKIT

Building skills in online tools for group participation is essential for executives. *Mural* is a good choice for group collaborations. *Zoom, Teams,* and *Google Meet* all have polling functionality that allows leaders to assess group responses and check in about current dilemmas.

The biggest issue for leaders when it comes to online meetings is to remember to look into the camera as they speak. Doing this means they are effectively looking directly into the participants' eyes, which is more likely to generate a sense of personal communication. Only the most intuitive and astute leaders are able to sense individual responses in this type of environment. For most, this is a skill that needs development.

SEISMIC SHIFT 6: FROM BEING TIME POOR TO THRIVING WITH HEART OF THE MATTER DISCUSSIONS

Time is wealth. Time is a priority. The greatest lever executives have to control their time and the efficacy of their relationships is to master brief, purposeful interactions and to choose where they will focus their time. Many executives I meet have regular "catchups" with their direct reports. Rarely are these valuable, because they tend to focus on the wrong things. Too often, the focus is on listening to their team members report and discuss results, rather than discuss whatever is at the heart of the matter. Invite your reports to give you a weekly email update with three categories:

- Five-six results they have achieved (not activities)
- Risks and alerts and how they are managing them
- Focus for the upcoming week

This brief weekly email from each report provides three insights:

- It alerts you to what's being achieved in your overall group
- It enables you to see any gaps or overlaps
- It helps you and your team members identify what's at the heart of the matter you'd like to discuss

In addition to identifying the outcome for each discussion, you'll gain several hours each week that you can put to better use.

CONCLUSION

Marianne Williamson wrote in *A Return to Love*, "Our deepest fear is not that we are inadequate, our deepest fear is that we are powerful beyond measure." Leaders, this is your choice. Small actions have powerful impacts on relationships and results. Most of the seismic shifts outlined here require leaders to shift from ingrained habits which are failing to produce lively productive meetings, to brief thoughtful preparation. Implement any one of these and your capacity to lead powerful meetings dramatically increases. Implement each of them and you will transform your organization.

WORKS CITED

1. D. Jones, *Leadership Material: How Personal Experience Shapes Executive Presence*, Boston London: Nicholas Brealy, 2017.
2. C. E. Ackerman, "What is attachment theory? Bowlbys' four stages," *Psychology Today*, 2020.
3. C. Hazan and P. Shaver, "Love and work: an attachment-theoretical perspective," *Journal of Personality and Social Psychology*, vol. 59, No. 2, 1990.
4. A. Mehrabian, *Silent Messages: Implicit Communication of Emotions and Attitudes*, Belmont, CA: Wadsworth, 1981.
5. L. Perlow, C. Noonan Hadley and E. Eun, "Stop the meeting madness," *Harvard Business Review*, no. July, 2017.
6. P. Lencioni, *Death by Meeting: A Leadership Fable...About Solving the Most Painful Problem in Business*, San Francisco: Jossey Bass, 2004.
7. A. Hollo, *From Impossible to Possible; Two Simple Rules to Assure Exceptional Public Value*, Maryborough, Victoria: McPherson Printing, 2018.

8

Building Collaboration and Commitment—Not Compliance

The smartest people are constantly revising their understanding, reconsidering a problem they thought they'd already solved. They're open to new points of view, new information, new ideas, contradictions, and challenges to their own way of thinking.

—Jeff Bezos
Founder of Amazon

We are fooling ourselves if we accept that binary decisions, yes or no, underpin significant business successes. Executives' decisions are far more nuanced. We need to stop glorifying objective rational executive decision-making and start accessing the experiences of team members, so that decisions are pragmatic and enduring, while also creating alignment and business progress. In this chapter, we'll look further at the tools you can use to work well in groups, build worthwhile interconnections among individuals, and get the outcomes you want.

Frustration in executive teams often results from executives not being heard. They feel their views are dismissed or not taken into account. Meeting preparation is focused on content, rather than exploring implications for the business.

How are decisions made in your organization? Is it by the loudest voices, the majority, or the boss making unilateral decisions? Who influences whom? Are decisions made outside of the meeting? Few decisions are yes or no. Decision-making is nuanced with a wide range of perspectives around any leadership table. How do leaders draw these out and have confidence their decisions will endure?

DOI: 10.4324/9781003167334-8

"Take two minutes and turn to the person next to you" is one of the most maligned and poorly used directions given to groups. It's there to give the group facilitator breathing space to gather their thoughts. Rather than having crafted an invaluable purposeful conversation among two or more peers, group leaders use this direction to selfishly focus on themselves.

Here's a better alternative that's more likely to draw out thoughtful contributions: *"Talk in two's and threes. Discuss your response to what you've heard so far. Then let us hear what resonates in this proposal, and how we can address any gaps."* With this option, you can now have a valuable conversation. Your work as a leader is to continually stimulate and access the group's intelligence.

FROM POLAR OPPOSITES TO ALIGNMENT THROUGH CONTINUUMS

Too many leaders rely on their own ego and intellectual ability to contribute ideas and opinions in decision-making. Too few rely on their instincts, intuition, and trusted relationships, alongside empirical data.

A better way to do this is to use the continuum as a tool to look at the range of perspectives for significant decisions. Continuum-based decisions allow leaders to assess:

- The range of current positions within their group in relationship to polar positions in a pending decision
- The views and perspectives behind the current positions
- The movement toward or away from polar positions, as people are influenced by hearing others' perspectives and seeing others' positions

Let's look at a leadership team assessing its current strategy.

The question asked was *how confident are you that our strategy hits the mark in our current context.* The polar positions are yes—I'm confident and no—I'm not. Their leader gives the direction to stand up and take a position that best represents your view—closer to one option or the other. Immediately, the leader and everyone in the group can see where each person stands. This gives them a quick sense of whether or not they're on track.

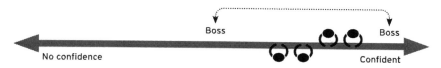

FIGURE 8.1
The confidence continuum

The leader has a range of options, depending on the outcome wanted from the ensuing conversations. They can make the decision based on the data before them, or they can choose to hear from everyone (Figure 8.1).

I coached a senior leadership team that was responding to major developments in response to context demands. We redefined the team's purpose, role, priorities, success measures, and values. The final document was ready.

I wanted the team to assess how confident they were that what they had identified would ensure their success in leading and embedding the upcoming changes. I placed a 17-feet sticky tape line on the floor to set a continuum which ranged from *no—not at all* at one end to *yes—completely* at the other. I invited executives to stand on a point on the line which reflected their confidence. The CEO stood up firmly on the yes end. Other team members were gathered closer to the 80% point on the line.

I asked the executives, what would get them to yes. Ted wanted to wordsmith the document. This behavior with the group had held the team up in earlier decisions. I knew to trust the method I was using. The CEO immediately moved to below 50% on the line. A second executive, Jim, said he also wanted changes. I asked what were the changes? Jim wanted to move the two result areas relating to staff to the top of the list. Ted wanted three specific wording changes. These were proposed and rapidly agreed upon. A third executive made the updates on the document. Within two minutes, the document was finalized, accepted, and every executive—including the CEO—was at yes. Job done. Seeing and experiencing the nuances of others' responses physically impacts leaders' interpersonal senses and helps clarifies their expression (Figure 8.1).

To access the range of views, the leader's invitation is:

Let's hear from each of you how you came to take this particular position on the line. This allowed the group to hear how solid their strategic foundations were—or not.

If the group was spread unevenly along the continuum, the leader should ask, *what should we be doing to bring you closer to yes?* This helps uncover what would be needed to get back on track. The responses then shape the group's agenda and priorities going forward.

Two features of this method stand out. Physically taking a stand in relation to others helps clarifies people's thinking. They are not just sharing intellectual ideas or concepts around a table. They see before their eyes in the present moment the impact of their contributions on others through their physical responses. Group members are aware of one another's positions. Alignment and divisions are displayed for everyone to see, and executives are better able to work with what is in front of them. Everyone has more information and a deeper understanding of the drivers and compelling interests of others in the group.

Using the continuum in decision-making helps leaders and groups assess their confidence and satisfaction in their own performance as a leadership team, whether it's refocusing marketing strategy, driving productivity, or deciding how to grow a customer base.

STORYTELLING

Stories are powerful people connectors. Personal stories give insight into a person's life beyond their job role. This alone stimulates the imaginations of listeners. In addition to facts and experiences, stories convey values. Listeners connect emotionally with the values conveyed—or not.

> Jill knew her staff criticized her for micro-managing. She had heard her one-on-ones were "inquisitions" and some of her staff didn't feel trusted. Jill was defensive and invited me to help her with this situation.
>
> It turned out that Jill had become too close to the results she wanted and too distant from her staff. They perceived her as critical (which

she was), and she perceived them as not up to her standards. On the surface, the relationships looked positive. In reality, the tele relationships were mutually negative. The gap between Jill and her staff had widened. I coached Jill to tell her own story to warm up the group before having the conversation about micromanaging.

Jill began with: *"How does a girl from a dysfunctional rural working-class family become the lead influencer of sector professionals in Australia, you might ask?"*

She said there were three areas where she regularly focused and invested:

- Developing relationships with the people around her
- Taking time to understand how things worked
- Being reliable

Jill told the group what she had learned from her chaotic family, since as the eldest she had to be responsible for her siblings.

She said she chose her career path because she inherited a sense of social justice from her mother. Her mother would invite waifs and strays to live with them. When she was younger, Jill couldn't understand why her mother did this. She remembers becoming furious with her mom. They had little enough as it was, and they were then asked to share what they had with these strangers. But Jill said she came to realize the lack of fairness for those who are disadvantaged, and she was driven to make a difference. This early experience shaped her entire professional life.

Jill told the group she realized she was overfocusing on how work was done rather than results. She wanted to hear what motivated each of her staff to make a difference. Then she wanted to hear what they wanted to discuss with her.

As Jill moved toward her staff, they moved tentatively toward her.

Notice how in her story, several simple sentences convey significant insights and observations.

Three steps and one principle will help you effectively tell your own story.

The Steps:

- Lead by self-disclosing a personal fact from your experience or with an insightful question.
- Add three lessons you've learned.
- Conclude with a personal insight that connects you and your audience to the current situation.

The principle: Keep your story brief, succinct, and relevant. Leaders make a mistake when they tell their whole story at once. Every leader has many stories to tell, and multiple opportunities to tell them.

My long-time colleague, poet Maris O'Rourke, tells storytellers to think of their lives as an ocean. Dotted throughout are islands. Imagine each one of these islands as the significant people, events, and moments in your life. Take five minutes to note ten of these images. Share two or three with the group. Now, write for five minutes about the first one. *What happened? How was this experience? What did you learn? How is this relevant now?*

My own approach is to use sociometric criteria as questions to elicit stories for the purpose of people presenting themselves simply and powerfully. This allows others to get to know them rapidly, beyond their job function. Many examples are threaded throughout this book. Others include:

- **Think about a turning point in your life.** Where were you? What was happening? What were your choices? Your decision?
- **Get together in groups of three**. Let the others know one area in your current work where you have mastery and another area with which you're struggling.
- **Think of a moment when you first realized you were a leader.** *Where were you in the world?* Identify the precise location, e.g., London, Riverside on the Thames close to the Tower Bridge, in Norton Rose Law Firm. *How old are you? What was happening?*

There are three central tenets of storytelling in interpersonal settings:

- With groups of more than nine people, don't have each individual share their story to the wider group. Be selective. Choose one or two. Avoid repeating privately what has been said. Encourage participants to keep asking one another these questions to build their relationships.

- The intention of sociometry is to enable people to build relationships so that they work better together. Don't focus on solving a business problem in these conversations.
- Don't document these stories for any organization record. Their purpose is solely to build relationships among staff, bosses, and colleagues.

Leaders continue to draw us into their stories. The storyteller becomes accessible and human. Their insight helps us make connections with our own lives and work, and frequently gives us hope that anything is possible. Group members can put themselves in the leader's shoes. Their experience creates a deepened understanding and creates a sense of belonging for others. This in turn dramatically increases interactions and cohesion among group members—enabling work problems to be more easily discussed and resolved.

INTERVIEWING TO FIND COMMON GROUND

The best method for people to get to know one another is through interviews. Questions can be used either in two-person groups within team meetings, triads in larger groups, or during coffee breaks or online mini conversations. Interviewing or sharing stories expands peer perceptions. Here are guidelines for this approach.

- Only ask questions to which you are also willing to respond.
- Focus on listening to the storyteller, not warming up to your next question.
- Three questions are enough for any interpersonal session; one is sufficient for a larger group session.

It is essential to let participants know nothing will be recorded and anything discussed will remain confidential.

BUILDING RELATIONSHIPS INTERVIEW QUESTIONS

Here are some sample sessions which you can use to begin team meetings:

1. What makes you jump out of bed in the morning? What concept/person/result really motivates you in your work?
2. What do you hate the most about work? How does that affect you? How do you manage that?
3. What are you most satisfied with in your life? What lifts your spirits when you're low?
4. What is your biggest frustration right now?
5. In which recreational activities do you participate? e.g., family, friends, movies, theater, sport, unusual holidays.
6. What are your core values? What's really important to you and why?
7. What are some of the groups or people who are important to you?
8. History and geography: Where were you born? What school(s) did you attend? How was school for you?
9. What irritates you the most regarding organizational life?
10. What or who makes you happy?
11. What were you doing seven years ago? What do you imagine you might be doing in seven years' time?
12. How do you see yourself as a member of this senior management team? What is the main role you take within groups/teams?
13. What are three strengths you bring to this team?
14. With what work situations do you have trouble and why? How do you feel when faced with them? How do you tend to handle them?
15. What new things have you learned in the past few years and how are you applying this? What are you learning at present?
16. What has been the most difficult experience you have faced as a leader and what did you learn from that?

USING SOCIOMETRIC CRITERIA TO BUILD GROUP RELATIONSHIPS

Assisting your team to build interpersonal connections for team cohesion is even more important in the post-pandemic world. The pace of organizational life has sped up tremendously. Teams are now more likely to be formed for specific outcomes than to enhance a formal structure. Strategy is more likely to be 12–18 months out, rather than 5 or 10 years. Given this, it's important to find multiple ways to strengthen relationships rapidly among team members.

There are three types of criteria for interventions which enable participants to build relationships to facilitate their work:

- Investigate what currently exists within the group.
  Where are you within the family birth order and what influence if any does that have on you as a leader?
- Focus on actions that are relevant to the immediate dilemma at hand.
  Who in our group do you think has working solutions to what is in front of us? And how could you assist them going forward?
- Identify strategic relationships which will benefit the business in the future.
  Which is the one key strategic relationship that you could make, strengthen, or turn around right now, that would make a rapid positive difference to our business?

CAPTIVATING PERSONAL OR BUSINESS INTRODUCTIONS WITHIN TEAMS

Plan to spend about six minutes per person on each of these types of introductions.

Participants:

- Name, role, the business outcome of your day-to-day work.
- A little background: companies for which you've worked. Explain what you loved or what you hated.
- A difficult thing you've been through and what you learned about yourself from that experience.
- The legacy you want to leave from your work in this group.

Business Leaders:

- The purpose of the group
- Three results I'll deliver by year end

- The three main challenges with which I'm grappling
- The help I'd like this year
- Four skills, abilities, and attributes I have to offer
- My most annoying trait
- The best way to work with me

Logistics: Appoint a timekeeper to give a one-minute-to-go signal. Invite one person to manage the themes, trends, risks. Give a two-minute summary after every four presentations.

BEING RUTHLESS IS GOOD

Leaders—you're much too polite. You need to learn how to interrupt. Interrupt team members if they speak for longer than two minutes in your meetings. Interrupt people who drone on, are unfocused or off topic, ill prepared, pontificate, make sweeping statements, or indulge x-factor unfounded predictions. Learn the distinction between interrupting and talking over someone. Avoid the latter.

Let me interrupt you. What is the main point you want to make?
Let me break in here. Thank you. Now let's hear from someone else.

The biggest mistake leaders make in meetings is that they think they need to hear from everyone. Actually, the art is in choosing who should be heard. In groups of more than nine people, if everyone were to speak for only 2 minutes, any discussion would take 20 minutes or more. Executive teams larger than nine are committees—they're unworkable as a decision-making group.

REPORTING BACK IS USELESS

The worst invitation any group leader makes is to hear everyone report back from small group discussions into the larger group. The regurgitation of others' conversations is a time-consuming innovation killer. Skillful leaders who make an ancillary invitation after small group discussions take everyone into new territory. Here's a typical invitation: *In threes, discuss your responses to the proposal. Then report back one action we need to take as a leadership team to capitalize on this opportunity.*

In large meetings (15–30 people), if you believe hearing from five executives would give adequate perspectives on a new initiative, use polls to ask which people the group wants to hear speak on that particular topic.

PROCESSES FOR PARTICIPATION

Once you've established why—your purpose for any conversation—you can decide on the best process for participation. The quality of question you generate dictates the depth of experience and quality of ideas contributed from participants. Here are some ways to invite contributions:

- Ask who is going to begin. Set a time limit. When they've finished, ask who will be next.
- Note each participant's name and make a check once they've contributed so that you may easily see that everyone has participated. Summarize and offer a next step.
- Invite one person to speak, then suggest they invite the person they'd like to hear from next.
- The least preferred process is to go around the group in seated order. This is known as "creeping death." You know the inevitable is going to happen: it'll be your turn next. Most people are too busy thinking about what they're going to say rather than listening to other contributors.
- Start with whomsoever has the first birthday in the year.
- Work in alphabetical name order.
- Choose the most alert-looking person to begin. *I'd like to hear from you first, Claire.* Then, let the group decide who will be next. Don't be fazed by silence as people think and digest what they've already heard. I rate silence highly and favor silence over people jumping in and cutting off others.

CONTROL THE CONVERSATION

Purpose is everything. This means right down to deciding the purpose of each agenda item in meetings, and every interaction you have. Leadership teams are better prepared in meetings when they clearly know whether they are sharing information, updating context, having a discussion, sharing stakeholder information, shaping wild ideas for innovations, or making a decision. They have crisp discussions, are more likely to make rapid decisions, and are confident their meetings move the business forward.

Precision gains commitment and focus. When crafting your questions, e.g., know whether you want to hear executives sound out implications for their divisions, for implementing strategy, for organizational capability, or something else. Be precise. Vague invitations like *"let's hear your feedback"* elicit vague responses.

SUMMARIZING

If it's not you as the leader, have someone who is a skillful and trusted summarizer. Choose an individual who can appreciate and name conflicting perspectives, create vivid images, and have a strong sense of group process with the next steps they propose.

A powerful summary goes something like this:

> *We have four conflicting positions on the table. We've hit a brick wall. To move forward, I propose we have each position present for three minutes about how adopting their proposed solution will leave our customers in a much better state. Now, who's up first?*

This is the moment when leaders need to look ahead to see who is at the table with them. There are many factors leaders rely on in making decisions; empirical evidence is only one. Others are insight, intuition, gut instinct, knowledge, experience, and foresight, and your trusted colleagues and bosses. Whom do they trust to make decisions which will progress the business? They may disagree on the decision being made, but once it's been made, you want their total buy-in to what's been decided.

MEETING DISCIPLINES

The senior leadership team mentioned earlier in this chapter were so unclear as to when they'd made a decision that they didn't implement any decisions at all. All topics for decision were taken offline and those decisions were made bilaterally between the general manager and the CEO. This created a mystery about who really knew what was happening. They would seemingly reach agreement, then immediately move into their next unrelated conversation. I coached each manager to say, "That's our decision." This gave the secretary time to record the decision accurately. Up till then, the leaders had behaved as if the CEO was the decision-maker, and they were the helpless harpies, hammering home what was needed.

In addition to the six keys of Chapter 7 for powerful meetings, here are four meeting disciplines:

1. **Ensure you know the outcome** you want from each discussion. Then describe the improved condition of the business, stakeholders, and/or customers, for example, how they will be better off after this.
2. **Verbally repeat the decision** once it's been made. Ensure the note taker has an accurate record.
3. **Avoiding asking for your peers' opinions** when you want something to occur. Be bold and make a proposal. Declare your position. Say what you want using the pronoun *I*—whether you are the leader or a participant. Don't hide behind questions as if your boss or peers have the answers. Embed "*I* want us to ..." and "*I* propose we ..." into your vocabulary.
4. **Interrupt rapidly** and talk to the whole group when discussions or a contribution goes awry. Be firm and pause the conversation. "*Stop. Hold it. I want to make an observation. We're all over the place in our discussion. Some of you have a lot to say, others are quiet. Some of you come unprepared, others are prepared. Each and every one of you brings valuable experience, knowledge, and ideas and I want us all to have access to them. I want our meetings to be purposeful and really impact the business. I want us to improve the lives of (insert). I want to be in a group that can discuss difficult things and make decisions which improve the condition of (insert). I want you to stop making one*

another the enemy when you disagree. I want each of us to accept we have tough things to discuss and decide, and that we can do this well.

"I want to hear briefly from each of you. Firstly, I want to hear one thing that would dramatically improve our meetings. We will choose the top three items and implement them. Then we'll reassess again in four weeks. So … who is going to begin?"

When you speak in this way, you own your authority and accountability. This allows you to share your vision, direction, and expectations for the group.

Next, set a task at the end of the meeting:

To strengthen the relationships in this group so that we can have robust conversations and make inspired decisions, with whom would you choose to meet and have coffee (or Zoom with) in the next few days?'

Review the outcomes in your ensuing meeting.

LIGHT, DARK, AND NO SWITCH AT ALL

There are three types of people in meetings:

- Those who bring *light* and add value to the relationships, conversations, and decisions
- Those who draw the attention of the group into a *black hole*
- Those who forgot to activate the "on" button and are *neutral* and contribute nothing

WHO ARE YOU WHEN YOU TURN UP TO LEADERSHIP TEAM MEETINGS?

In Chapter 9, we'll examine the wide range of ways in which leaders can contribute and influence in groups. For now, let's review the notion of lateness for meetings. These two things don't go together—ever.

Ensure you build a reputation of timeliness in beginning meetings. Reward those who arrive on time. Don't repeat what's been already discussed for latecomers. Everyone has made a choice whether or not to be present. Repeating what's already been covered is insulting to those who were there from the start. It's up to the latecomer to join the group ready to add value and work. Anything less isn't acceptable.

For in-person meetings: Enter the room and be engaged. At a minimum, look at everyone as you enter the group and say, *Good to be with you.*

For online meetings, send the same chat message to everyone just before you turn on your video.

PLEASE, NO APOLOGIES

Apologies are a social nicety when you've caused significant emotional hurt, or unwittingly crossed a personal line within business relationships. The inference is that you are not likely to repeat that behavior. Apologies from the habitual latecomer are a waste of everyone's time. Social niceties and work don't mix.

Apologies draw attention to the apologizer and take attention away from the work of the group. No excuse or explanation cuts the mustard with leaders. Everyone is busy and each individual made a choice to prioritize this meeting. If you, the group leader, are late, tell the group, *Carry on, I'll join shortly.* Then be engaged from your first moment of entry into the room.

Online meetings are similar. Join the conference with your microphone on mute and be ready for action. Look at everyone through the camera and smile. Send a group message: *Good to be with you all, I'll comment shortly.* Any executive who crashes into a meeting late, forgets to mute, allows background noises to dominate, then takes their time to be settled, is in the wrong meeting. More likely, they're in the wrong role, or even in the wrong organization. This is made worse by the comment, *I haven't had a chance to read the meeting materials.* These tone-deaf behaviors drain the life blood of any meeting. Be in that group of people who add value to every meeting by being prepared and contributing succinctly.

PUT AN END TO MINDLESS REPORTING

Reporting results to leaders in one-on-one meetings is a time-consuming process. The only reason to report results in meetings is that everyone knows what's going on, the status of projects, and the impacts on the business. My best advice to leaders from Chapter 7 is to have your executives prepare a brief simple weekly email report with their top five successes and achievements, two or three risks and alerts and how they are being handled, and their focus for the coming week.

This brief email gives leaders an oversight of all the action in their group and enables them to focus in one-on-one or in team meetings on the things that matter. Leaders have far greater control over their time and where they put their attention. They can then focus on improvements, fixing gaps, and addressing risks or alerts with which they should be familiar. Report writers have an ongoing sense of their achievements, and the key conversation they want to have with their leader.

A second option is the brief weekly standup (15 minute meetings with participants standing together). The purpose of this meeting is either stakeholder intel and/or to know who needs help and who can offer help for the week. Or problem-solving. *Directions:* Stand in a circle, ask each person to briefly outline their most difficult issue. Ask if anyone can help with that—if it is you as leader say what you'll do and by when. If it's someone else who offers help, then ask them what they'll do and by when. Keep the meeting short and focused on knotty problems and solutions. Do not make these meetings *information only.*

DEBRIEFING FAILURES AND FRAUGHT PROJECTS

Any debrief which includes what worked, what didn't, and what's next needs to be thrown out the window. These questions draw superficial responses and fail to engage participants in a meaningful way. Encourage authentic responses by drawing out the responses of key players. Use these questions:

- What was your most satisfying experience with this project?
- What helped achieve that?

- What frustrated you the most?
- What lessons do we want to embed for the future?

Forget recommendations. They hold little personal ownership and accountability other than for the writer and are rarely implemented other than for compliance.

THE CHASM EMERGES AND THE LIFELINES ARE DOWN

In my career, I've only met two people who were really masterful in resolving conflict, but I know dozens of leaders who are good at causing conflict. I've seen hundreds of leaders procrastinate when faced with a difficult conversation. I also know many leaders who love to be blunt. Being blunt only works within trusted relationships, and then only some times.

Inevitably, you'll enter dangerous territory. The chasm will emerge between you and your team, or within your team, and the lifelines will be down. How do you communicate tough news, maintain positive relationships with those with whom you must communicate, and still ensure the outcomes you want? What do you do?

You know these leaders: *I just want to be honest* or *I'm going to tell it like it is.* They're life's blunt truth speakers. The trouble is this doesn't work. Something crucial is missing. The reality is the hard-hearted blunt truth speaker has sacrificed their relationships. They reject the other person or have no interest in them. Their flow of feeling is negative. In the interests of truth and honesty, they've stepped away from being collegial, compassionate, or caring. The likelihood of their message being received as a scorpion's sting is high. The likelihood of them being a relationship developer is zero.

Successful leaders know how to:

- Focus their communication on their relationships. This is not about pleasing the recipients. It's about leaders understanding the impact of their interactions on others, and how the recipients feel about that.
- Metaphorically or literally stand in the shoes of the recipients, look at the impact of the decision through their eyes, and imagine the implications, perspectives, and subsequent feelings. They literally

reverse roles and see the world through the eyes of recipients and tailor their communication accordingly. They do this by returning to their own role and communicating this with fresh understanding.

Some might call this empathy, but it's more than that. This is leadership at its best. The effect is that recipients feel understood and accepted. There is no judgment. By reversing roles, the leader actively strengthens the mutual positive tele relationship with their group. Without a positive flow of feeling any attempt for leaders to reverse roles is experienced by recipients as a manipulative technique.

I once observed a leadership group cover their substantial business agenda with collegiality and collaboration. They had mastery of their content amid a fast-paced series of items, ranging from a business-as-usual round table identifying likely pressure points to the timing for integrating several new general managers into the business. Over the course of two hours, the CEO provided a masterclass as meeting chair. Everyone contributed information and expertise. They made progressive suggestions and rapid decisions as they carved their way through the seven major items, including four presentations.

Suddenly, a presenter cut across and contradicted the CEO. The *blunt truth speaker* had arrived. The damage was done. The CEO became terse and combative. The leaders looked at their papers or laptops. The air was electric.

At that moment everyone in the room, including me was on red alert. You know that moment when you know to tread carefully. We all silently raced to justify our role in what had transpired. It was time to take a deep breath, and warm up to the importance of building the working relationships again—to back down from fight, freeze, or the desire to run the other way.

The blunt truth speaker had no positive effect.

The only way forward was for one of us—any one of us—to lead as the *relationship developer*. What wasn't said and needed to be was:

Our working relationships are important to all of us. We have tripped and fallen. This last part of our meeting was terse, and we were all part of it. Right now, it would be easy to be defensive or criti-cal with one another. We have a glitch. Let's keep in sight all we have developed and regroup.

Then a fresh conversation as colleagues could be had.

There are at least three options available to us, including when we might take this action:

1. **Ask a question**. *What is one action each of us can take to get us back up and running again?*
2. **Find the cause**. Identify what caused the blunt truth speaker to contribute, then fix that. In this example, the likely glitch was in commissioning the outcomes the senior leadership team had sought.
3. **Let the moment go**. You can be confident this behavior will be repeated when everyone is feeling more resourceful.

CONCLUSION

Leading and aligning groups doesn't happen by accident. In most cases, leaders have been carefully prepared, and decided to learn the processes of fail-safe group beginnings and structured conversations. They have a strong sense of the dangers inherent when things go wrong in groups and have accessed a range of methods to manage their emotional responses to the inevitable frustrations.

9

From Dysfunction to Impact and Influence in Leadership Teams

In *Three Keys to Faster, Better Decisions*, Aaron De Smet, Gregor Jost, and Leigh Weiss said:

> *1,200 managers across a range of global companies gave strong signs of grow-ing levels of frustration with broken decision-making processes, with the slow pace of decision-making deliberations, and with the uneven quality of decision-making outcomes. Fewer than half of the survey respondents say that decisions are timely, and 61 percent say that at least half the time spent making them is ineffective. The opportunity costs of this are staggering: about 530,000 days of managers' time potentially squandered each year for a typi-cal Fortune 500 company, equivalent to some $250 million in wages annually*

[1].

So it's likely that managers at a typical Fortune 500 company may waste more than 500,000 days a year on ineffective decision-making. To stop this financial, time, and expertise waste, leaders must step up as both direction setters and the tuning forks shaping both how they themselves and others contribute. Gaining alignment is a relationship process, set in motion by leaders, including the way they themselves behave in groups.

One thing that continues to surprise me with senior leaders is how many do not contribute to senior leadership meetings. Having worked with thousands of leaders, I notice typical behaviors—and one of these behaviors is to remain silent in meetings.

DOI: 10.4324/9781003167334-9

Of course, there are many reasons for their silence. Leaders are put off by:

- Absence of meeting protocols result in others either talking frequently or for long periods—adding their contribution is a challenge
- The meeting atmosphere is competitive
- The purpose or outcome of conversations and meetings are unclear
- Others have already made the point they were going to make
- They think others have more important roles than they do, or that peers do not want to hear what they have to say

Others perceive non-contributors as either arrogant or *know-it-alls*. They act as if they are above the conversation. Others again see non-contributors as disinterested or as not having anything relevant to say. In contrast, some fall into the trap of overcontributing and have something, at times irrelevant, to say on every topic, and then some.

Many of these excuses are untested assumptions. Mistakenly, many leaders associate these with their own lack of confidence. I see poor relationships and inadequate meeting management as probable causes.

Most of leaders' work is in groups, yet other than in the 1960s, there is little group-work training embedded in leaders' development.

How do you influence leadership teams? There are at least nine ways I have outlined below. Successful leaders use many or all of these regularly.

NINE WAYS TO POSITIVELY IMPACT LEADERSHIP TEAM MEETINGS

1. Share Your Content and Your Expertise

Many of you will have been subject matter experts in your careers and know you are masterful in contributing your knowledge and expertise. You know stuff.

Three main downsides of overusing your expertise to influence are first your direct reports are disempowered. Their talents are most likely underutilized. Second, if you tend to take offense when your boss or colleagues disagree with you, or when they focus on the practicalities of alignment and implementation, you "lose." Third, you are likely to be absolutely "right'" in your detail, but your peers or boss may disagree with you. They may prefer alternative solutions. If you persist, shut out alternative views, and refuse to inquire "why do you think that?," you risk destroying your relationships and may be seen as a logic bully [2]. Successful experts learn to think from a range of perspectives, not just their own.

Two tips for subject matter experts on senior leadership teams are to:

- Discuss the implications of applying your and other's expertise to shape quality decision-making
- Teach your staff how to think about the implications of using their expertise

2. Be an Astute Context Reader and Direction Setter

Senior leaders' vital ability is to read the continually shifting contexts they are in and to know how to navigate the way forward. Without astute reading of current context, organizations lose market share, stakeholder relationships weaken, and staff deliver services or products that are neither relevant nor timely.

There were failures to read the rapidly shifting context in the early days of COVID-19. Many supermarkets shifted to "click and pick up," yet customers had to wait days for their pickups to be ready. Other companies offered online deliveries, but courier companies were overloaded. Some items took weeks to deliver. In contrast, successful companies in the early days of COVID-19 lockdowns were the ones who offered preconstructed boxes of groceries with emphasis on swapping in and out goods, rather than buyers choosing every item. Amazon responded astutely to the pandemic by opening 100,000 new positions across their fulfillment and delivery network. They then created 75,000 jobs to respond to customer demand. They took on staff furloughed from other companies. They removed over half a million offers from bad actors looking to exploit the crises. Jeff Bezos and his leaders read the rapidly shifting context, anticipated, and delivered [3].

3. Use Insights from Your Experience

Everyone's eyes roll when a leader says, "When I was in ABC company we …"

A leader who learns to share their leadership practice and perspectives in compelling ways have the pathway to influence. Impactful leaders describe their learning from key events: "I learned that if I continually ask how people are feeling, and what they are noticing during change projects, our chance of successful implementation skyrockets."

Amazon founder and former CEO Jeff Bezos' insight into the success of having a network of physical stores with low capital, high returns, and meaningfully differentiated customer service unlikely underpins Amazon's e-commerce success [3].

4. Be Future Focused with Your Vision and Direction

(Vision + direction + results + expectations) × repeatedly = Alignment and results.

Compelling leaders share their vision and direction and the results they want often. Their most frequent phrase is "What I want … this phrase is an expectation and invitation—people respond."

Vision, direction, results are sought and expectations embody the central function of leading. In a world of continuous change and developments, successful leaders share vision, hold to it, help navigate, and clear the inevitable roadblocks and use the central functions to align others. Too many leaders find it easier and "safer" to delve into everyday details and be distracted by operational urgencies. They forget their vision—if they ever had one in the first place.

The leaders' role is to create the future. They do this by sharing their vision and direction frequently.

Alex was appointed Head of Department to a college art department. He was frustrated. This was his first leadership role and his vision was for his staff to stop focusing only on implementing the curriculum and shift to a primary focus on strengthening each student's identity and their self-expression through art. At the time, his decisions with his staff focused on responding to their requests for computers for photography and heating for classrooms. He now wanted each of his staff to focus on the students' needs enabling their identities as indigenous students and artists to flourish. Alex had no idea how to do this and invited me to coach him. Over the initial weeks,

Alex shared his vision relentlessly. Writing the Annual Report for the board, usually an onerous individual task, he invited each of his team to contribute two things they had done which resulted in the students' flourishing, and to identify one area for their future focus. He ensured each of his staff call each student by their first name. He displayed the students' art throughout the school, and in the Annual Report. He ran staff meetings where his team outlined what they noticed worked for students to rapidly expand their talents. By year end, Alex and his team were delighted with the students' results. Alex had an aligned team. I asked him if he were to look back at himself this time last year, what guidance would he have given himself? He outlined three things:

1. Don't be afraid to say no
2. Trust your gut
3. Make the decision

He went against his habitual nature to avoid conflict and learned to say, "What I want you to do is ..." To his astonishment and delight, his team would respond positively to his direction.

Alex saw that relentlessly repeating his vision for the students, and following through with his team, both individually and as a group, were the aligning factors for his team.

The top organizations I work with invariably align three key elements: vision, results, and right relationships.

By right relationships I mean teams which ensure both their internal connections and their stakeholder relationships are fit for purpose. Many teams have two of these three elements—the secret to success is in aligning all three (Figure 9.1):

1. Teams with a clear vision and key success factors produce an unforgiving group culture. There is little appreciation or vitality among team members.
2. Teams focused on vision and ensuring the right relationships create a truly feel-good culture. People love working in these teams and

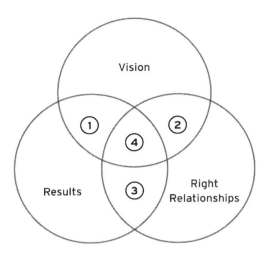

FIGURE 9.1
Transformative top teams

are inspired by both their purpose and one another. They have great discussions; however, there is little action and fewer results.

3. When leaders emphasize right relationships and results, a productive team ensues. This team is typically hardworking yet without a vision, the people are easily exhausted.

4. Teams aligning vision, the right relationships, and results are transformative. These teams have a clear direction, produce exceptional results, and create satisfying productive work cultures.

5. Keep the Group's Eyes on Results

Leaders who share results positively impact groups. These are reminders of what leaders have set out to do and how they are accomplishing these goals. Rather than being swept up by the inevitable day-to-day urgent matters, they focus on progress and achieving targets. Great leaders' focus their conversations on creating the future not unraveling the past.

Start meetings with *"Let's hear from each of you, one thing you are proud of this week, and one thing you are grappling with."* Results bring optimism to groups. They are your success measures. Don't take them for granted.

Improving your organization's and customers' conditions is your raison d'être. Don't take your or others' results for granted, or tuck them away for the outdated performance review discussion. Keep them alive every day especially when times are tough. Know where your and others' silver linings are.

Executives who describe activities bore people.

Contrast *"We interviewed four people for the new group manager role this week"* with *"We had four exceptional choices for the group manager role. I'm confident our appointee will turn things around rapidly."*

Contrast *"We continue work on improving systems"* with *"We retired fourteen (14) complicated workarounds and have returned these processes to four simpler states! Our output has trebled."*

6. Be an Insightful Navigator

How often are you in meetings littered with red herrings and conversations that head down rabbit holes? How often are you frustrated by your peers being poorly prepared or refusing to engage in progressive interactions?

Essential to every leader's toolkit is the capacity to observe the process they are in, participate simultaneously, and be the process navigator when things go awry. One metaphor to assist *insightful navigators* is *to be on the balcony then shift to the dance on the dance floor.* This enables you to:

1. Have insight into what is occurring
2. Look up to see where the group needs to head
3. Decide what will help the group get there

This third step is showing the pathway forward by navigating the contributions needed. I am not talking about the solving of business problems here, I am championing providing a process for participation (Chapter 7) to help people know how to participate relevantly when things go awry.

Navigating is essential when a group is going around in circles or a group member has gone down a rabbit hole or is diverting with curve balls. Address the whole group, share your insight on what is happening, and reset the path forward. *Remind the group of the outcome being sought, and the expertise they bring, and suggest, let's hear briefly from those who have yet to contribute, what is most important for you?* Simple directions work best.

Insightful navigators make offers which progress the work of the group. They know what needs to happen, succinctly articulate this, and offer to lead or produce what is needed.

Leading through conflict is not the time to be unprepared. Navigating conflict by having a strategy for moving forward is essential.

"Out beyond the ideas of right-doing and wrongdoing, there is a field. I will meet you there. It's the world full of things to talk about" [4].

There is no difference today. Leaders don't lead transformations any more than they can lead a river. What leaders have to do is learn to navigate the rapids.

Here are some tips for resolving the inevitable conflicts that arise.

The key principle of handling conflict, including at a distance, is as follows:

Have a plan. Always have a plan. Certain sequences work better than others. This is not the time to trust in your intuition or your old ways of doing things. Without a clear plan, and clear purpose, things will not go well.

If you want to be a successful conflict navigator, there is a structure to follow. This helps both you and everyone stay composed (Figure 9.2).

a) **Open with mutual benefits** that help the person/group know that you have their interests at heart.

b) **Say what you observed.** Avoid blame, assumptions, and interpretations. *"I have noticed that …"*

c) **Acknowledge what you did or didn't do** that might have contributed to the situation.

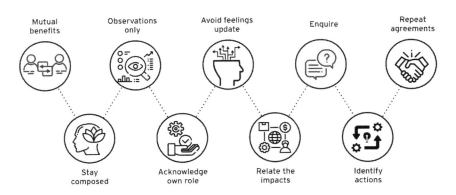

FIGURE 9.2
Always have a plan

d) **Avoid feelings updates.** Your feelings are simply impacts based on your interpretation. They may change as you start to understand the other's perspective.

e) **Relate the impacts** of their behavior on you, or anyone else in the organization.

f) **Ask** what they were aware of.

g) **Identify actions.**

h) **Repeat** what each of you are prepared to do differently going forward. "I am now going to summarize. We have agreed that from now on you will … and I will …" [5].

7. Use Personal Insights Astutely

Another significant shift leaders can make to their contributions is from being *silent astute observers* to provide their insights on what is happening within the organization, context, progress or implementation, strategy, or the myriad of organization matters.

Leaders need to master the art of being in two places at once. How is this possible, you might ask. Not only is being in two places at once actually possible, but it is essential for any leader. The capacity to reflect, form insights, and then act on those insights is a basic tool for anyone who wants to be effective with groups. This capacity is known within group-work training as the *participant-observer*.

Ron Heifetz, Alexander Grashow, and Marty Linskey [6] noted that as participant-observers, leaders can be on the dance floor, move to the balcony to see what is happening, and then return to the dance floor with new patterns of moves that are both meaningful and relevant. They can discuss strategy and relate it to immediate operations. Looking at balance sheets, leaders can review details in spending aberrations and signal implications for fraud, or uncover dramatic savings. These leaders detect red herrings, malicious interactions, and unhelpful interpersonal conflict in meetings. They intervene to bring conversations back on track or to propose a process that draws in relevant contributions.

Being an *observer-participant* changes the focus of leaders from working in a linear fashion to observing patterns. Stepping back out of the action enables the leader to reflect, generate insights, and then rapidly act on them. Historic leadership metaphors talk about taking a helicopter view—the view from the hills versus being down in the weeds, similar to the balcony and dance floor analogy noted earlier. While being *observer-participant* is an essential leadership capacity, this behavior doesn't survive on its own. The capacity helps the leader make observations, develop insights, and take action on their insights. Yet, this is also not enough. This doesn't explain why people disengage from their leaders.

What really causes people to disengage from their leaders, and vice versa?

There's a simple response to this question: it depends. Staff engagement depends on:

- How much a leader's content or agenda dominates their interactions
- How much a leader's followers have the capacity to choose how they participate
- How well the leader "reads" the mood of the people they influence
- How well the leader communicates vision, direction, and expectations

Hearing "What strikes me here is ..." is an excellent opener to sharing insights and implications for progress and outcomes. Your insights can be from any one of multiple perspectives: a personal perspective, your business group perspective, an organization or sector-wide perspective, or a client, a stakeholder, or the disenfranchised perspectives. Insightful leaders are perceived as thoughtful, wise, and generous. Too many leaders are confident sharing their insights interpersonally but fail to back themselves when they are in groups. I've met many who open doors for others when they dare to share their thoughts and insights. The organization is better off with their contributions.

8. Be Sure to Champion Others' Contributions

Leaders who notice and champion the contributions they see others make contribute directly to building bridges across business groups. They take responsibility for the development and visibility of others. One leadership team I worked with was in dedicated silos, causing duplication, repetitive problems, and interpersonal frustrations.

I proposed they begin each of their meetings by sharing what they had noticed someone in a peer's business group do and achieve. In a short period, appreciative alliances were built among the leaders. This led to rapid intergroup problem-solving and speedier decision-making in the leadership team.

Each time I consult with long-time CEO clients, they inevitably introduce me to several of their staff. *"Meet Amrita, she is our ABC, and she is doing the most amazing work in helping us achieve JKL. Or meet Bill, he recently joined my leadership team. He has dramatically upped our capacity for trusted stakeholder engagement."* These introductions let the individuals know the CEO notices their work, give me insight into current updates in the organization, and provides links to whom I might talk to down the track should I want to.

9. Move Appropriately from Silence to Collaboration, and Alignment

If all else fails, the easiest way to contribute positively to leadership teams rather than being silent is to let your peers know when your thoughts align with theirs. In leadership teams that share stakeholders and customers, thinking will align.

Instead of thinking, "that's my view, too," or "someone already said what I was thinking," add "I am with you on that." Let others know you share their perspective or agree with what they are proposing. When your view is contrary to what is being proposed, "I disagree" is powerful. Avoid being oppositional. Be curious, "Do you want to know why?"

Letting others know what you think and feel on important matters is more likely to create collegial alignment in any group than remaining watchful and silent.

THE FIVE KEYS TO POWERFUL INDUCTION

Leaders continually have opportunities to share their vision, shape direction, and create alignment. Integrating new team members rapidly is yet another opportunity. Existing team members might well be uncertain and have fears of how much are these newcomers going to "renovate the house" that they have been working so hard to build.

Leaders have five keys to ensure new appointees are successfully and rapidly inducted into their leadership team, the business group, and the organization by making clear:

- Their name and role
- The main impacts the leader wants the person to have

- The reason why they chose this person
- Three or four qualities or experiences the leader knows the individual will bring to their work
- How they want the team to work with this person

This simple format ensures the best entry and rapid acceptance of any newcomer. Hearing the leader's reasons for their choice clarifies the vision for both the role and the individual involved. Leaders who overlook or avoid this process watch informal connections emerge based on nebulous pecking orders. The integration of the new executive is haphazard and the chance for rapid alignment is lost.

Being publicly recognized and championed by your boss is a powerful experience for anyone. Anyone who has presented to an audience and had a poor introduction knows the hard work of building a strong relationship with their audience. Similarly, with entering new groups. Leaders' have another opportunity to supercharge their team into collegial action and alignment.

MEMORABLE OFFBOARDING

In addition to any formal farewell, or instead of, personal acknowledgments are powerful. I'm not talking about speeches or stories. I advocate simple heartfelt appreciations from one person to another in a group setting. I am advocating personal acknowledgments; a series of adjectives expressed in two or three sentences beginning with "What I have appreciated about working with you is …"

Whatever the reason employees leave your organization, knowing their contribution was valued builds their reputation and yours. Specifically who to involve in this process is the most significant factor. For staff leaving in positive circumstances,

1. In a team meeting
2. Invite each person to comment "What I have appreciated about working with you is …"

Enough said. This results in moving personal tributes. As leader your role is to keep breathing, have some tissues handy, and listen carefully.

For staff leaving under a cloud is similar. Invite a close colleague to choose four or five people who have positive regard for the leaver to contribute as above. Avoid people who want to "make a point" or are negative in any way toward the individual. That will have been covered formally.

EVOLUTION OR REVOLUTION—KNOW WHERE THE LANDMINES ARE

As a developer of groups, learn to read your leadership team's progress, and identify areas for improvement. This keeps you and your team familiar with their progress, builds a vault of positive experience, helps each person shape group culture, and keeps your learning edges in mind. Once you have mastered this process, invite team members to do the same.

Practice Session: Take ten minutes alone at the end of one of your meetings to reflect:

- What five words best describe the emotional tone of the meeting as the group gathered?
- Make six observations of any meeting; include three things that worked well
- What five words describe the emotional tone of the meeting at various points
- Make three insights for improvements

Practice this relentlessly for four months and focus on implementing the recommendations for improvements.

ASSESSING TEAM PROGRESS: ON-THE-BALCONY TEAM OBSERVATIONS

There are a myriad of observations points for leaders and their team members to be conscious of how well they are working together. Listed below are team tasks for post-meeting reflections and conversations:

- What two or three interactions (what was said and done) were turning points in the group's progress?

- What interaction deepened group member's authenticity?
- What two or three interactions pulled the group *away* from the outcome being sought?
- What insights do you have to assist this group to develop?

Here are three examples of meeting observation reports I complete for clients at the conclusion of observing their meetings; one early in the team's development, the second three months down the track, the third one month after that. In the interim, my work with the team is building their interpersonal relationships and working with their development agenda. The three-part formula is:

1. The emotional tone of the meeting
2. Six observations
3. Two to three recommendations for significant progress

EXAMPLE REPORTS

Track this teams' development by comparing reports over a four-month period. Notice the organic development of this senior leadership team (Table 9.1).

PRESENTATIONS THAT HELP
EXECUTIVES MAKE DECISIONS

By now you will have accepted the idea that leading is the relationship business. In Chapter 4, I give five steps for powerful presentations. If you want your leadership team meetings to sing, ensure any and every presenter has your song sheet. Ensure they know the outcome you as the leadership team want from having them at your table. If you fail to do this, you can guarantee three things:

1. Decisions won't make sense
2. Random ideas will divert attention
3. Executives leave your meetings with their valuable time wasted

TABLE 9.1

Comparative Team Development Reports

Senior Leadership Team Meeting Notes 1	Senior Leadership Team Meeting Notes 2—Two Months Later	Senior Leadership Team Meeting Notes 3—One Month Later
Emotional tone:	**Emotional tone:**	**Emotional tone:**
Tentative, friendly, apologetic for late start	Purposeful. Succinct, intelligent, insightful, focused, light-hearted moments	Thoughtful, succinct, informative, collaborative, decisive, terse
Observations:	**Observations:**	**Observations:**
• Group members were unprepared for agenda items	• Very strong chair kept things focused	• Executives organized and personable
• Contributions were convoluted and detail-focused	• Dramatic increase in crisp interactions	• Dramatic increase in crisp interactions
• Outcomes of agenda items unclear	• Decisions/actions "disappear"	• Collegial and clarifying in discussions
• Discussion emphasis not decisions	• Discussions become vague and purposeless with descriptions, explanations, or leaders being philosophical on how thing could/should be	• Everyone had a sound grasp of financial detail and implication
• Several conversations taken offline for bilateral decision	• External staff contributor's interactions were exemplary for clarity, intention, and outcome	• This was a masterclass SLT meeting and decision-making
• Contributors from outside SLT well-prepared and helpful		• One presenter had unclear purpose and outcomes and subsequent interactions were terse and combative
Recommendations:	**Recommendations:**	**Recommendations**
• No apologies, come prepared to participate	• Leader to close off discussion and confirm decision	• Brief presenters with the specific outcome you want from their interactions with SLT
• State the outcome you want from each agenda item	• Stop descriptions, explanations and philosophizing, stay future focused	• Establish how we "recover" when we are knocked off balance
• Be brief and succinct	• Keep the interactions mutual	

I've observed leadership team meetings, where the presenter

- Apologized as they had only been in the job two days, and weren't on top of the material someone else had prepared
- Apologized as they had prepared the presentation for another group, not the one they were presenting to
- Didn't acknowledge the underworked set of slides with confusing text and graphics
- Had four stated outcomes for their presentation, yet not one of them aligned with what the leadership team wanted

And then there was the meeting where leaders didn't know where the paper had originated or what problem it was trying to solve. There was no leadership team owner of the paper. Everyone thought one of their peers had commissioned it with the CEO. No-one had.

This is madness and has to stop.

Presenting to the senior leadership team is both a sought-after experience by professionals and direct reports, and they find it anxiety-provoking. Everyone wants to do a good job. No one wants to be in a meeting where the cringe factor is high with a poorly prepared presenter, or an underworked paper. No one wants to be on the receiving end of an inquisition. Make the relationship between presenters and senior leaders strong, purposeful, and inspiring. Make commissioning work and implementing results your leadership team's art form. A 6-page well-worked document with an executive summary trumps 20 pages of poorly focused ramblings any time.

SEVEN WAYS TO ROCK THE PRESENTATIONS WITH YOUR LEADERSHIP TEAM

1. Have a senior leader who has a good relationship with the presenter or the topic as sponsor. Sponsors welcome the presenter, make sure there is a place to sit if in-person, and admits them to the room if online.
2. Have the leadership team's clear purpose and outcome of any paper/ presentation. Ensure the paper's purpose indicates who will be using

the material to make decisions. The sponsor ensures the outcome the presenter wants from their presentation aligns with the senior leadership team's desired outcome.

3. There is an agreed format for any paper or visuals, e.g., six pages/slides maximum of well-worked narrative with a front page executive summary outlining both the purpose of the paper, the outcome/decision being sought, and the improvement to the business or the significant value add to customers and/or stakeholders.

4. Warn presenters that their time is likely to be halved. I have been in too many meetings where a 20-minutes presentation is in fact 10 and presenters are ill-prepared to adjust.

5. Ensure you hear the presenter's exquisite question prior to the meeting, and adjust to ensure the outcome will be achieved and the talents and experience of your team are well utilized.

6. Debrief with the presenter on the impact of their presentation on the team and the decision along with your appreciation.

7. Stipulate the working method of every paper commissioned is either:
   1. A high-quality completed paper, or
   2. Developed as an iterative and organic process. Writers consult with specific key others as they go, so there are no surprises for decision-makers, or
   3. Needing a major rework after a designated consultation

CONCLUSION

Leading businesses is demanding and complex. There is no reason for leadership team meetings not to be purposeful vibrant events for everyone involved—the leaders included. Everyone involved deserves to be part of stimulating work conversations that grapple with the challenges that inevitably arise. Most people give more attention to creating social events than they do in producing stimulating satisfying work meetings, including who is invited.

It is too easy to be diverted by the administrative details in setting an agenda, taking minutes, or with online technology than giving thought to the outcomes you want from each item, how to tap into everyone's expertise, and how every conversation you participate in will progress the business.

WORKS CITED

1. A. De Smet, G. Jost, and L. Weiss, "Three keys to faster, better decisions," McKinsey Quarterly, May 2019.
2. A. Grant, "The science of reasoning with unreasonable people," *The New York Times*, 31 January 2021.
3. J. Bezos and W. Issacson, Invent and Wander; the collected writings of Jeff Bezos, *Harvard Business Review*, 2021.
4. Rumi, "Persian poet and Sufi master," 12th Century.
5. C. Williscroft, *How to Handle Conflict at a Distance.* [Interview]. 15 April 2020.
6. R. Heifetz, A. Grashow and M. Linskey, *The Practice of Adaptive Leadership*, Boston: Harvard Business Press, 2009.

10

Press the Release Button Before You Get to the Trip Wire

It may appear that people in groups behave in ways that are irrational and illogical. That isn't true. What happens is that when people aren't respected, don't feel their contributions are valued, or believe they are patronized or dominated, they find many ways to rebel.

Leaders can communicate respect and value through simple processes based on how relationships develop. By implementing a few of the relationship disciplines in how groups work, leaders produce inspiring vibrant meetings.

POWER AWAY FROM HABIT

To power away from habit, leaders can experiment and be impacted by the results. In the early 1900s, Pavlov discovered dogs' conditioned responses to certain stimuli. Similarly, the experience of success is a powerful motivator for leaders repeating new behavior. Relationships are refreshed, the flows of feeling are realigned, and new neural pathways are generated. This is emotionally based learning generated from integrating experience.

Leaders, you have an extraordinary challenge. Your mission, should you choose to accept it, is to relate to large groups of people while personalizing your interactions. This is indeed an art form. You do this by creating mutuality—your positive flow of feeling oriented to creating a better future. You do this with language, by using principles and processes of accepting and including others and having them know they, too, influence what happens.

DOI: 10.4324/9781003167334-10

FINE-TUNING IS ENOUGH

For many of you reading this book, fine-tuning how you relate to groups will be enough. Take any of the processes here and implement them. At a minimum, become adept in creating exquisite questions or have several elegant processes for participation and you will dramatically increase purposeful participation. Implement the six principles for powerful purposeful meetings and be amazed by both your business results, rapid confident decision-making, and new talents released by your employees.

Implement all of them and you will transform your organization and life. Problems and challenges won't lessen, but you and your team will be more likely to go home at the end of each day and week refreshed and ready for evenings and weekends.

If you haven't already mastered listening, now is the opportunity. Listen to gain insight. Listen to accept a range of perspectives. Listen to become a masterful summarizer.

THE PERSONAL ELEMENT OF PROFESSIONAL DEVELOPMENT

It's not possible to work with people and groups without attending to your own personal development. Your personal values and mindset shape your behavior. Examining and reassessing personal values and mindset is integral for leaders to work well with groups.

My own professional development training was in psychodrama, which is a group learning method. Assessment and accreditation are by peers and a Board of Examiners. Strong peer relationships are central to personal development, as are good working relationships with authority figures.

I had to learn how to have both. I had to learn how to have relationships with peers where I had authority over them, and with those who had authority over me because of our roles within the organization. I had to learn the distinction between being authoritarian and being authoritative. I had to learn how to participate in groups without being the leader. I had to learn how to intervene in groups without taking over from the leader. I had to learn to read my relationships and know how to adjust my behavior to remain connected to people. This development is definitely not for the faint-hearted. Purpose, trust, vulnerability, and the ability to apply insights come to the foreground.

For you, reader, your personal development path may differ. If you are continually frustrated, ask yourself: Why is this? Where did you learn that as a response? If you cut people off, ask: Why is this? Where did you learn that as a response?

You get the picture.

If you notice you are cynical and negative, have you rejected curiosity, and narrowed down from whom you take advice? Have you become isolated or self-sufficient? Would you benefit from greater courage to live your dreams of working well in groups? How much does your reputation for leading inspiring meetings mean to you? Are you someone who tends to look out for others, but has too few people looking out for you?

Keep refreshing your *psychological social atom*—those people you confide in and who confide in you, those people who look out for your best interests, and would do anything for you.

Your psychological social atom is the smallest number of people with whom you have an emotional relationship in order for you to maintain your social equilibrium (Figure 10.1) [1].

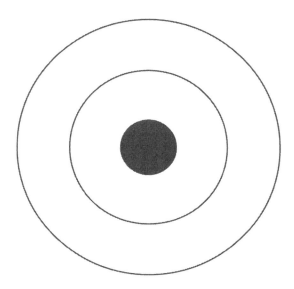

FIGURE 10.1
Your psychological social atom

Practice Session: Put your name in the center, using distance to represent current closeness, and identify colleagues *whom you choose,* with the following eight criteria:

- Among my friends and colleagues .... would be concerned if I was stressed and upset
- I feel I can confide in .... about almost anything
- I would drop everything to listen to ....
- .... helps me see the funny side of things
- If I were lonely, my first thought would be to seek .... out
- .... would drop everything to listen to me when I needed help
- I feel responsible for ....'s well-being
- It would be hard for me to be motivated without ....

REFLECTIONS

- What do you notice?
- What gaps or overlaps do you see?
- Do you rely on too few people with these criteria?
- Which criteria might you use to develop more relationships?
- Whom will you choose?

Action: How might you strengthen your psychological social atom?

Ignore your personal development at your peril. Without your genuine imperfect self as leader, implementing the processes in this book will be seen as just a set of administrative techniques. No one wants to be on the receiving end of an impersonal technique.

There is little value in making accurate assessments of problems in your organization without implementing solutions. Incredible technological advances in Artificial Intelligence, driverless cars, vaccines, online meetings, and space travel don't, won't, or can't replace the power and impact of inspiring human relationships.

Learn how to lead and work well with groups in a basic human capacity.

WHAT ARE YOUR OPTIONS?

Coaches, mentors, and psychotherapists all over the world are familiar with the relationship between personal development and the professional capacities of working well with groups. Leaders who use curiosity and inquiry are able to set development goals without knowing how they will achieve. They find out what has worked for successful colleagues. They discover experts with whom they want to work. Annoyingly, for corporate executives, one size does not fit all.

BEGIN WITH THE END IN MIND

The only way to really know you are successful is to have simple clear success indicators. What would you want to see as a result of developing your capacities? Here are success measures identified by some of my best clients:

- Staff members see the leadership teams members working in groups of two and three.
- Staff members contribute readily to business improvements.
- The leadership team has a reputation for well-run collaborative meetings with the right people involved in decisions.
- Leadership team members consult with one another and decide on contentious matters prior to coming to me as CEO or to leadership team meetings.
- Interactions of the leadership team are reported as inspiring, productive, and worthwhile.
- The culture survey results later this year will reflect significant improvement over last year's results.

Each of these is easy to measure. You'll know when you're successful and the value added to your organization is sizable—if not in specific financial returns, then in developing a reputation as being a great place to work.

It doesn't matter where you begin. What matters is that you, as leader, start to shape your leadership team through five interrelated areas (Figure 10.2):

1. Refresh interpersonal relationships for cohesive behaviors to ensure decisions are made, owned, and implemented.
2. Clarify and agree on the purpose, role, success measures, priorities, and values of the leadership team.
3. Make the shift from silo-driven discussions to discover the real leadership team agenda where your executives are contributing their best insights and expertise to the group or organization-wide.

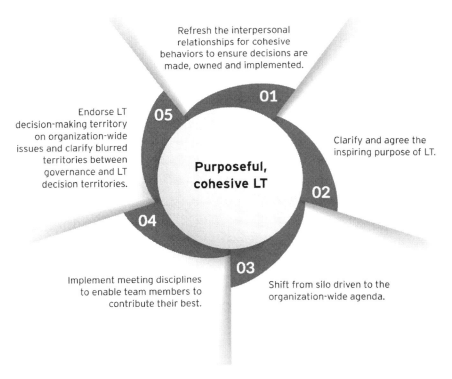

FIGURE 10.2
Five interrelated areas of leadership team development

4. Implement meeting disciplines emphasizing the purpose of the meeting and the outcome you want for each agenda item. Enable team members to contribute their best with exquisite questions shaping discussions and a clear process for participation.
5. Clarify your leadership team's decision territories, including with your governance structure. Blurred decision territories create frustrations and bureaucracy and slow down decision-making. Eliminate these.

EARLY INFLUENCES HAVE LASTING EFFECTS

Who would have thought the family dinner table could dramatically influence a leader's ability to lead and participate in groups?

This one microcosm of early life—repeated over days, weeks, months, and years as we grow up—has significant influence on how leaders behave in groups. Around the family dinner table, you either conversed easily as a family and learned to disagree without offending others, or you remained silent as one parent or both dominated.

In my recent work with leaders, we discussed turning points in their careers. One leader shared a moment of boldness early in her career, when she fearlessly disagreed with a leadership team. The group listened and were drawn to her.

I asked her, *"Where did you learn that?"*

"Each evening meal, my family would discuss what was going on in our lives, and as I grew up, we debated current social issues," she explained. "Frank and fearless discussions come naturally to me."

I sensed intrigue in the group, so I directed, *"Step forward if you had dinner table conversation in your family."*

Six of the eight stepped forward, and looked at one another in recognition. I invited the two who had not stepped forward to share their experience. Both had experienced silence at the meal table. No one was to speak during the meal.

This was familiar to me. With my own upbringing, we were expected to be silent during dinner. My dad would come home from work and want quiet. I could barely sustain this and would burst out laughing, which meant I'd be sent to my room without my dinner. Repeatedly. My mother would secretly bring me something to eat later in the evening. This experience sparked my fascination with what was really happening in groups and who knew what was happening. I longed to learn how to create group settings that were satisfying and worthwhile.

School and graduate college were similar. The teacher had the floor. Contributing was not encouraged. To participate, questions were designed to elicit knowledge. Imaginative responses were not invited.

Like many executives, I learned to participate in groups as an adult.

Don't wait until you hit the trip wire and things go badly wrong. You can gain mastery of the levers for alignment and engagement with those with whom you work. There are a myriad of release buttons available throughout this book for you to use. Take hold of them—make them your own. Become masterful in creating leadership dynamics that drive success in your organization.

As we come out of a once-in-a-century pandemic, we need to realize that there will be no "new normal." We are *there* now. Two things remain unchanged. First, leaders will be continually leading through events they had not previously encountered. Second, their main work is to drive vision, direction, and expectations, and to create inspired invitations for their people to participate.

FUTURE TRENDS

Here are my nine predictions for the future of leadership teams:

- Demand for well-led, purposeful, interactive online, and in-person group experiences will only increase.
- Intact leadership teams will be relics of the past. Expect some leadership team members to change each year. Become skilled at onboarding and farewelling team members.
- Leadership teams will rely on short-term pop-up groups based on clear and specific outcomes with handpicked contributors.
- Commissioning work and implementing results from these groups will become your leadership team's art form.

- Groups who function with clear purpose and outcomes will have briefer meetings and make faster decisions.
- Fresh new voices will shape innovation and business direction—leaders without formal titles will emerge. It will be critical to base your decisions on intuition and trust backed up by data and insights.
- Influential leaders will rely on their abilities to develop and maintain high trust relationships not trending influencers.
- Successful leaders will personalize their interactions.
- Successful leadership teams will rarely be larger than eight people.
- Purposeful small group interactions among two to four people within larger meetings will become normal in progressive boards and companies.
- Technology will not replicate genuine, trusted human interactions.

FINAL WORDS

I've been asked my thoughts on the differences between leaders of today and leaders of ten years ago. Today, leaders have strong self-insight, definitely know their added value, and have significantly better stakeholder relationships—each of which was sorely lacking ten years ago. What's remained unchanged is their hesitancy and inability to lead vibrant purposeful group interactions.

Two decades ago, I had the enormous privilege of being in a live presentation by author and consultant Peter Block, entitled *In Praise of Mediocrity*. There were more than a thousand people in the session. Two things stood out for me. One was that Peter championed fit for purpose over perfection. The second was role play we did in pairs. One of us was a loved and dying grandparent, and the second was our immediate self ... what would we say to the loved one in that situation? Two things struck me: First, all of us there got deeply involved with one another, audacious as Peter Block's invitation was; Second, how essential it is not to wait until the last moment to say and do what is important to you.

All the lights turning green, the stars realigning, and a measure of good luck would be good, but of course the best way forward is to let those around you know what you think and feel on important matters *now*. Do this in ways that will build your relationships, rather than hurting them. Now is your chance to enhance your capacity to be an inspiring leader of people by creating exceptional group dynamics.

REFERENCE

1. C. Hollander, and S. Hollander. *Action Relationships in Learning.* Denver, Colorado: Snow Lion Press 1978.

Index

Note: Page numbers followed by *f* and *t* refer to figures and tables